T0197230

Heart Swells

Essays and Inquiry for Self-Discovery

BRIGID LEA

BALBOA.PRESS
A DIVISION OF HAY HOUSE

Balboa Press books may be ordered through booksellers or by contacting:

Balboa Press
A Division of Hay House
1663 Liberty Drive
Bloomington, IN 47403
www.balboapress.com
844-682-1282

Because of the dynamic nature of the Internet, any web addresses or links contained in this book may have changed since publication and may no longer be valid. The views expressed in this work are solely those of the author and do not necessarily reflect the views of the publisher, and the publisher hereby disclaims any responsibility for them.

The author of this book does not dispense medical advice or prescribe the use of any technique as a form of treatment for physical, emotional, or medical problems without the advice of a physician, either directly or indirectly. The intent of the author is only to offer information of a general nature to help you in your quest for emotional and spiritual well-being. In the event you use any of the information in this book for yourself, which is your constitutional right, the author and the publisher assume no responsibility for your actions.

Any people depicted in stock imagery provided by Getty Images are models, and such images are being used for illustrative purposes only.
Certain stock imagery © Getty Images.

ISBN: 978-1-9822-4694-5 (sc)
ISBN: 978-1-9822-4693-8 (e)

Library of Congress Control Number: 2020917653

Print information available on the last page.

Balboa Press rev. date: 10/23/2020

To *you*, my fellow seekers.

Want

I wanted to be heard, so I truly listened.

I wanted to be seen, so I really looked.

I wanted to be happy, so I uplifted.

I wanted to be comforted, so I fondly touched.

I wanted abundance, so I gave of myself authentically.

I wanted to be full, so I embraced.

I wanted to be loved, so I opened to it all.

CONTENTS

Dear Reader,

This collection of essays is about frustrations and doubts, acts of faith, moments of inspiration, and experiences of grace that happen when you are seeking authenticity and peace. When I was in the midst of editing this book, my husband and I decided to get a divorce, we sold a house, I bought a house, I got a second part-time job, and my father passed away. These events delayed the publication of the book for over a year as I dealt with their inner and outer consequences. They were challenging and had much to offer me about how to live honestly, lovingly, and with integrity. These situations were very much in keeping with what this book is all about—how life happens and how we deal with it. It is about how our personal lives unfold as opportunities to find deeply meaningful answers to our longings, our desires, and our questions. These life opportunities open the heart to insight and healing.

This book is all about moments that have made my heart swell with the profundity of what life offers up. Through these moments, I have learned that the questions we hold—those that we initiate about ourselves and what is dear to us—are as deeply important as the answers. Answers flow from the questions. Questions are in direct relationship to free will. We only know that which we want to know. We only see that which we want to see. We only experience that which we are open to experiencing. Simply, our life experiences unfold the answers from our simplest to our deepest questions.

Life has taught me to be observant, to ask endless questions, and to be quietly patient and listen for the answers. (Please don't get me wrong. I am not saying I am able to listen patiently for the answers.) What complicates matters is that answers can be elusive because they do not always come in the form in which we ask for them. They may arrive in the form of a book or song lyrics, in the story of a child, from the warmth of the sun, in the way an animal seeks your company, within a text from a friend, or with an insight that arrives through meditation or contemplative thought. Answers arrive through paths of least resistance and through forms unique and special to each of us.

Yet the process of obtaining answers can be glaringly simple. The stories of our lives contain all the answers to our questions. The stories of our lives tell us our purpose. They are meant to uplift us, inform us, and set us free. *Stories are not meant to be held hostage, nor are they meant to hold us hostage.* We are not meant to hold on tightly to our stories. They teach us how to observe, learn, and grow. The key is to use them as momentum for living by flow rather than by force.

Some of the essays in this book cover simple moments, and some describe life-altering experiences, like my divorce. Regardless, they have all given me the opportunity to question, receive answers, and subsequently grow. By putting these essays out here for you, I will no longer hold on tightly to them. They are the result of a sincere quest for authenticity and an attempt to become more comfortable with my own sense of vulnerability. My hope is that the essays will provide stimulus for you to reflect on your life, ask your personal questions, and find your authentic self. May they give you guidance, or at the very least the feeling that you are not alone, as you open yourself to the answers your life offers.

Warmly,

Brigid

HOW TO USE THIS BOOK

The essays in *Heart Swells* can be read in order or by jumping around. The contents page lists the essays in order, but you may reference the index in the back if you are interested in finding essays that have a common subject or theme.

Following each essay is a page designed for jotting down your thoughts, insights, stories, reflections, and personal questions. Questions are the gateways to great openings. I have provided some questions after each essay to get you started. Feel free to use one, all, or none of them. They are meant to help you with your own self-discovery. If they aren't the right questions for you, these inquiry sections offer numbers without questions where you can insert your own questions. Following the questions is a blank, lined space for you to capture your creativity.

Take time to reflect on your questions, and look for both traditional and nontraditional answers. Some answers take time to develop, so don't be afraid to keep your important questions in the forefront of your life until such time when you personally hear those answers. Only you will recognize the right answers for you. You can always come back to the questions and add to your experiences and insights.

I encourage you to adopt a playful attitude and be gentle with yourself. My hope is that the examples in the essays will inspire inquiries for knowing yourself more closely, loving yourself more deeply, and healing yourself profoundly.

These essays can also be explored in a group context. In the back of the book, you will find guidance on how you might create a safe environment to explore what life offers. Our experiences are gifts to reopen at will and explore with more and more depth for our enrichment and healing. They are there for us until we are ready to release them. Whether you explore these essays and inquiries alone or in a group, it is important that you honor yourself and follow your heart.

Essays and Inquiries

Vulnerability

Honesty and transparency make you vulnerable. Be honest and transparent anyway.

—Mother Teresa

As I am writing this, I know that the outcome of my writing means too much to me. I want this to be something, or a means to something. That something is something more—to know my inner potential and live in it. Not just that, I want the journey of it, the feel of it, and the ownership of it. I want to know the difference between the half life I have lived and what it means to live a whole and complete life. Right now, writing this, I am the most real, most truthful, and most authentic I am ever able to be.

It scares me to death to put these things on paper and put them out in the world. So many times in my life, I have done this and have been slapped down and completely devastated. If someone recognizes this work, I may not be able to hide anymore. There are people I have hurt. So many embarrassing moments! Those moments are so personal and relevant to why I am who I am right now and why I know forgiveness is a real, living, breathing obligation for authenticity. To be authentic, you must be vulnerable. To be vulnerable, you have to risk embarrassment. I hate embarrassment! I hate being false even more.

I have never been intentionally false, ever. But I presented a mask to the world for survival. I learned to determine what people wanted to see and to hear, and then I was that as long as it didn't cross any of my moral or ethical lines. We may all do this in one way or another. But it got to the point where no one knew who I was. For me, it seemed like no one really cared anyway. Everyone is just trying to survive, and everyone just wants to be seen. Really seen.

How can you really be seen when all you present to the world is what you think it wants to see? Trying to live differently on the inside than on the outside will make you sick or addicted to something that dulls the pain. I have been addicted to safety, to my work, and to food. Meanwhile, my heart has longed for expression, kindness, and validation. It is willing to be vulnerable, to be embarrassed, and to be real.

Social science researcher and author Brené Brown says it eloquently in *Daring Greatly*: "Vulnerability is not knowing victory or defeat, it's understanding the necessity of both; it's engaging. It's being all in."

So here's to being vulnerable to life. Victory or defeat, I am now all in.

Vulnerability Inquiry

1. What does vulnerability look like for you? How do you avoid it? How do you embrace it?

2. In what ways has the pain of living superficially outweighed the risk of vulnerability?

3. What masks do you wear for survival? Do you still need them?

4.

Notes

_____

_____

_____

_____

_____

_____

_____

_____

_____

_____

_____

_____

_____

_____

_____

_____

_____

_____

_____

_____

Questions

Life seems to be set up around questions and answers. Therefore, they are the seeker's primary instrument for navigating and developing in the world.

Who is God? What is God? Who am I? What am I meant to do with my life? Am I living my best life? What is happiness? Love? What should I name my child so that she isn't teased her entire life?

These are big questions!

Questions that come from the deep desire for personal truth can change your life! Caryl Ann Casbon affirms that the questions we ask can and will inform and enhance our quality of life. In the preface to her book *The Everywhere Oracle*, she says, "Asking powerful, timely, clear questions is an art and a finely honed skill." Many times in my life, I have asked questions of life only to be continually frustrated by not hearing or, more likely, not understanding the answer. Often, I have asked a question and life has answered, but I have not gotten the answer I wanted, or I couldn't understand the answer because life answered with the truth, not what I wanted to hear.

Three things that I have found to be key in the relationship between deep questions and significant answers are patience, allowance, and awareness. Life seems to like a path of least resistance, so it may use things that one will most likely come in contact with in the course of daily living. For instance, I may wonder about how something like a water system works. Next thing I know, I see an infomercial on that very subject, or a friend introduces me to someone who works for the water department, or there is a book on water systems in the bargain bin, or a friend has to have a pipe fixed and informs me of the process.

Deep questions work within the concepts of free will, openness, and freedom. By asking questions, we invite life to work with us on things that are important to us, things we specifically want to know or address, and things that we are interested in. It is important that we be willing to receive once we have asked. We must allow the answer. Life will give us opportunities to open ourselves to answers we need, but it is up to us to invite them into our experience through our questions. It is a miraculous process, really—one that is certainly as much an art as a skill.

Questions Inquiry

1. What have been the big questions of your life?

2. What questions are you holding right now?

3. Have you received answers? How?

4. Do you feel that your questions are being heard?

5.

Notes

_____

_____

_____

_____

_____

_____

_____

_____

_____

_____

_____

_____

_____

_____

_____

_____

_____

_____

Beauty

For Christmas, my sister gave me a collection of flowering teas. It was quite a sweet idea. The tea buds are wrapped so that when hot water is poured over one to steep, the bud unfurls like a flower blossoming. The set came with a selection of different tea "bulbs," which were unique, pretty, and delicious.

Once I opened the set, we immediately had to try it out. It was fun to make the preparations, choose the tea, and watch the "flower" bloom in the clear glass teapot. My sister began rummaging through my cabinets for cups, and then pointed to the ones on the very top shelf. "We should use those," she said. Looking up, past her pointed finger, I saw that she was pointing at the cups from my wedding china. They were cups I had never used. I actually stated that out loud. She just said, "Yep." It struck me during this few-sentence exchange that this was a perfect use for them, which she already knew since she was pointing to them. She knew exactly what they were. Next to them was the Christmas china we had used only one time. My son, who was trying the tea with us, wanted to use a cup from that set. I couldn't understand for the life of me why we hadn't used these before.

I thought about this a lot later. Why do I isolate beautiful things like these for protection? They are on the top shelf so as not to get broken. They are never used for their intended purpose. I hate it when I feel I have no purpose or I am used for decoration. What moment was I waiting for if not for a moment like this, sharing a warm, comforting cup of tea with my beloved sister and son? Maybe this was exactly what I had been waiting for—for over twenty-two years, mind you. It struck me then that no moment is more precious than another. They are all precious moments.

My sister has gone back to Florida, but I still drink tea in those china cups to honor my sister, my son, my marriage, and all the precious moments that make up the day-to-day experiences of my life. How wonderful to have a reminder that there is so much loveliness already existing in our lives if we but notice it, take it off the shelf, and put it to good use. We all have things we hold in reserve for a more special time than today. But in reality, there is only right now. What better purpose can there be than to find comfort and beauty in simple things that are already within our reach? What better time than now?

Beauty Inquiry

1. What are you saving for a special occasion? Why?

2. What pleasures have you put on hold? Why are you waiting?

3. How do you experience beauty right now?

4.

Notes

_____

_____

_____

_____

_____

_____

_____

_____

_____

_____

_____

_____

_____

_____

_____

_____

_____

_____

_____

_____

4

Perspectives

Paco, our Chihuahua, weighs roughly ten pounds and stands roughly eleven inches high. He is always looking up. I don't know how he keeps from getting a crick in his neck. Paco is always begging to be picked up. It is as if he wants to see what everyone else sees. I got down on the floor with Paco one time just to see what his viewpoint really is: dust bunnies under the foyer table, legs of chairs, the doormat, and the baseboards. Not very interesting stuff, if you ask me. No wonder he wants to be picked up.

We also have a hawk that likes to cruise our neighborhood. It has a habit of landing on our mailbox post. The other day on one of our walks, Paco stopped and stared into the woods. He headed that way, but I called him back, then picked him up. A moment later, the hawk flew out of the woods and landed in the area where he was looking. What view did the hawk have of him, and of me for that matter?

Standing in the street, I got the sensation of Paco looking up at me and the hawk looking down at me—both perspectives real and correct, one not more right than the other. How grateful I am that this is the case. How dull the world would be if there was only one angle to perceive. How beautiful the diversity of our world is as seen through the eyes of our animals. Isn't this an essential truth? There are different perspectives. What we think is real is based on our perspective. If we understand that in its simplicity, does that not open the way to tolerance? For a peaceful world, is not tolerance of paramount importance?

To me, tolerance does not, in its essence, mean that we overlook differences. It may mean just accepting what is. But its ultimate value lies in embracing, celebrating, and affirming our differences with the secure knowledge that, as Maya Angelou said, we are more alike than we are unlike. Then, with that in mind, what's to fear? Ultimately, no amount of intolerance directed at me changes anything of who I really am. My hardest job in those moments of intolerance is holding on to the reality that what others think of me is really none of my business.

Now, I ask you, could we learn from the world around us, and in particular our animals, that there are many different perspectives, and therefore many different ways of seeing and being in the world? I believe the answer is yes, because I have gotten down on the floor and cleaned the dust bunnies. While down there, I made sure to leave some dog treats.

Perspectives Inquiry

1. How might you see life from a different perspective? How would this change how you view your world?

2. How has your perspective changed based on your experiences?

3. What would happen if you imagined yourself living another's life? How might you be changed or interact differently?

4.

Notes

_____

_____

_____

_____

_____

_____

_____

_____

_____

_____

_____

_____

_____

_____

_____

_____

_____

_____

_____

5

Quiet Support

My parents gave me a copy of the magnificent work *The Prophet* for Christmas in 1986. I had always loved poetry but not in the extreme. I preferred clever or witty poems to those historical or dry. Philosophical poetry is a class unto itself, and poet, philosopher, and artist Kahlil Gibran set the bar very high. I fell in love with his heart because it is in every line of *The Prophet*.

The book had to be timeless to speak to a middle-class white girl in Mississippi in 1986 when it was written by a Lebanese man in 1923. I was especially moved by Gibran's wisdom for parents:

> Your children are not your children. They are the sons and daughters of Life's longing for itself. They come through you but not from you, and though they are with you yet they belong not to you. You may give them your love but not your thoughts, for they have their own thoughts. You may house their bodies but not their souls, for their souls dwell in the house of tomorrow, which you cannot visit, not even in your dreams. You may strive to be like them, but seek not to make them like you. For life goes not backward nor tarries with yesterday.

> You are the bows from which your children as living arrows are sent forth. The archer sees the mark upon the path of the infinite and He bends you with His might that His arrows may go swift and far. Let you bending in the archer's hand be for gladness; for even as He loves the arrow that flies, so He loves also the bow that is stable.

I have read these words over and over in the last thirty years. It must have been these words that helped me navigate the proverbial road down which my sixteen-year-old daughter and I walked when she came home from a party late one night. It was the first big high school party she attended with upperclassmen. Most of her friends had been drinking. One of her best friends had cussed her out because she wasn't drinking with them. Yet she came home without having taken a drink. She told me about everything that went on. Somehow, I was able to simply listen and acknowledge her experience. I wanted so much for her to feel that she could trust and depend on me.

But I knew that I could not walk this walk for her. I remembered all too well being sixteen. I remembered that she came through me but she did not belong to me. She had to find her way, and she was doing very well. Anything I could say at that point would mess it up, make her question herself. She needed to know that she was strong enough, and to have me support that by not advising or even complimenting her. She was giving life to her own thoughts.

But what I could do was be the bow. I could be stable and listen, comment when she asked, hug her when she was down or frustrated, and give a little here and there to improve her flight.

Quiet Support Inquiry

1. Who has served as your bow?

2. Are you willing to take on the flexibility of being used by and for another's flight?

3. How have you supported someone by letting them be?

4.

Notes

_____

_____

_____

_____

_____

_____

_____

_____

_____

_____

_____

_____

_____

_____

_____

_____

_____

_____

_____

_____

_____

Home

Several years ago, I began hearing this incessant internal voice saying, "I want to go home." We all talk to ourselves in some shape, form, or fashion. Often, I would tell my inner voice to shut the hell up. And this statement in my mind almost became a mantra. Driving my car to work, I would think about what I had to do; then out would pop, "I want to go home." Picking up my kids, "I want to go home." Driving to the beach with my best friend, "I want to go home." It was unrelenting. So I had to look at it. Sure, I had some depression at times, but it wasn't like I just wanted to stay in bed all day long, in the fetal position with my covers over my head. I was out working, doing the family thing, and socializing. In spite of my "normal" life, the voice just wouldn't go away, so I had to look at it.

After two years, I found that the voice was not so much telling me to go home but calling me home. Turns out it was my authenticity, my inner self, or my inner light calling me to go back to myself—my true home. At the time, I didn't know how to do that at all. It was daunting. On the way to the beach one weekend, I spoke with my best friend about it. He said two very important things to me on that trip. One was that the most important growth experiences in life happen when you completely surrender to life (God, the universe, the Creator, et cetera). He said you have to put aside all fear of the outcome or the unknown and trust that life is working in your best interest. The second was that everyone's path is different. Everyone has to work out his or her own best way.

These things had depth and power to them. I went to a holy place (for me) in nature. Standing there, I prayed to the essence of life and said, with as much heartfelt sincerity as I could possibly muster, something to the effect of "If you will show me the way home, I promise I will go in the direction you point me." There and then, I committed everything I had in me to that promise.

Life could have zapped me with awareness, but instead, I was set on a path of gradual undoing. I have had to travel through some rough patches, and I continue to come across them as I make my way home. When I lose my footing or even fall, I accept that my direction is true, and I become lighter, more agile, and more patient. I still hear that internal voice. It is softer and less insistent. It is more like a calling than an insistent cry of longing. I know I am on my way.

Home Inquiry

1. What is your inner voice telling you? Is it helpful or harmful? How do you respond?

2. What is home to you? Where or when do you feel most at home?

3. What internal demons terrorize you, and how can you safely face them?

4.

Notes

_____

_____

_____

_____

_____

_____

_____

_____

_____

_____

_____

_____

_____

_____

_____

_____

_____

_____

_____

_____

7

Choices

The veterinarian in the town my husband and I lived in for thirteen years was amazing. She was both intelligent and intuitive. Never in my career have I seen anyone more meant to be a veterinarian. She lived for the animals. She was kindhearted to a fault.

When I was about to graduate from veterinary school, she offered me a job at her clinic. She presented me with a contract—a terrible contract. She said it was the first one she had had drawn up for anyone she wanted to hire. I won't go into details, but I will say I tried to get her to revise parts of it so we could reach a compromise. She wouldn't do it. So I had to choose whether to sign over the license and education that I had just spent four years and over $100,000 obtaining or to find somewhere else to work.

This was a very difficult choice. She was my mentor. The job was in my town. I had always had to travel long distances to work. I was ready to start a family. I had a huge school debt load, and this was a guaranteed job for when I left school. The hardest part was not knowing if I would lose a good friend if I turned down the job.

I really, really sat with this and deliberated over it. In the end, I turned down the job. I *knew* it would not be the right thing for me. But that threw me into a world of uncertainty. I was graduating without a job and with an unknown future. Fear and anxiety set in.

At graduation, I met the president of the veterinary alumni association. He was a very nice man who had a practice about eighty miles from where I lived. We talked for a while before we had to go in for the hooding ceremony. His role was to introduce us graduates to the alumni association and give us a graduation gift as we left the stage. When I crossed the stage, he handed me a lapel pin with my name on it and leaned down to whisper, "Why don't you come see me sometime?" Just that.

I did. He hired me to do relief work. Basically, that means that I relieved him from work so he could take time off. He was in a solo practice, so he needed an occasional half day off. About six months after I started working for him, I got a call from the health department. I had worked for them before and through veterinary school as a nurse. They offered me a job. This job had not been available when I got out of veterinary school. It turned into a full-time job. It led to the full-time job I have now.

If I had taken that first job, I would not have had the wonderful opportunities that I do now. I would have been locked into a rigid contract with limited outside experiences. It turned out my destiny was to work at the state level with lots of different people, travel in my home state and all over the country, and meet lots of different people from lots of different backgrounds.

We all may face times in our lives where we will have to make a choice based on what we feel is right even though we do not know the outcome. This is our leap of faith. My choice brought me where I am today, with a unique career and unique challenges. Your choices, too, have brought you right where you are. Every day, we face choices that can change the course of our lives. Every day, we have an opportunity to choose based on fear or what is in our hearts. These are the choices that determine the paths of our lives.

Choices Inquiry

1. What choices have been instrumental in your life? How have they informed you in making other choices?

2. What are or have been the consequences for not following your intuition or heart?

3. What choices do you need to make now to follow your heart?

4.

Notes

_____

_____

_____

_____

_____

_____

_____

_____

_____

_____

_____

_____

_____

_____

_____

_____

_____

_____

_____

Cardinals

If I had to choose, I would rather have birds than airplanes.

—Charles Lindbergh

So many things in one's physical life serve as symbols with deep meanings for personal enrichment. Cardinals have a special place in my heart and are one of those symbols for me. Not only are they beautifully distinctive with red coloration and a crest, but they also have a lot of personality. I often see them around my home in pairs or groups. Male and female cardinals share the workload of raising their young. They remind me to live life colorfully and treasure my companions. But it wasn't until a few years ago that they really became a personal representation of connection and love.

Spice, our pretty little female Dalmatian, got old and had to be euthanized. Her death affected me pretty deeply. I had rescued her while I was in veterinary school. She had been extremely shy. We took walks every day. I taught her to fetch; it was obvious she had never played before she lived with us. By the end of veterinary school, she was sleeping on my bed at times. However, Spice really liked to sleep in her very own crate. After veterinary school, she stayed out in our backyard during the day; where she had lots of room to move around, and then she went into her crate in the garage at night. Spice loved her crate because she knew she would get a treat when she went into it. Often, she would sleep in her crate whether or not she got a treat. We always had a strong connection, so I knew when it was time to ease her suffering.

A special thing happened not long after Spice died. One morning when we opened the garage door, a beautiful female cardinal flew in and landed on Spice's cage. This was significant for two reasons. First, a bird had never before flown into the garage. Second, we had more than one dog crate in the garage, and the cardinal landed specifically on Spice's.

For a long time after that, I saw cardinals almost every day. They would often fly near my car as I was driving place to place—close enough for me to see them but never close enough to get hit. Spice died over five years ago, but she is in my thoughts every time I see a cardinal. So not only do I get to enjoy the beautiful cardinals, but they simultaneously remind me of Spice and the special bond that can happen between people and their animals.

Although it is extremely sad to let go of a beloved pet, I am always so thankful to have had them in my life. When they come into my life, I know that they will not live as long as I will and that I will be saying goodbye. The prospect of giving my heart away to animals that will take it with them often causes a momentary hesitation. But they give me so much love during the journey that the hesitation is never enough for true resistance, but a moment to accept the inevitability of an ending in every beginning. But even in saying that, I know that it is only an ending to temporary physical existence. The cardinal reminds me that love doesn't die; it is ever present in this moment by simply remembering it and bringing it fully into the present moment.

Our lives offer us many moments in which to find comfort in symbolism. Birds are often thought of as symbols, such as eagles for patriotism and doves for peace. But anything may be used in such a way. For instance, certain foods trigger memories of loved ones who have cooked them for us or joined us at the table for time well spent. I find that realizing such symbolism is a playful, meaningful way of looking at life and a way of engaging all who interact with us in it.

Cardinals Inquiry

1. What are the symbols in your life that comfort you or remind you that life and love are eternal? How do you embrace them in this present moment?

2. How does having loved deeply show up in your life now?

3. Do you have the courage to love fully, knowing it may only last a season?

4.

Notes

_____

_____

_____

_____

_____

_____

_____

_____

_____

_____

_____

_____

_____

_____

_____

_____

_____

_____

_____

9

Phases

No matter what you see and hear from truly peaceful people, they didn't start out peaceful. They did a hell of a lot of work to get there. Obviously, it was rewarding work, but I can tell you firsthand that this work isn't easy. The path to peace can be quick or slow, but no one has the same time frame. I have come to understand that peace happens in phases. It is more about what you lose than what you gain. The more anger, depression, anxiety, and pain you release, the more peaceful you become. We often don't know how much progress we have made along the path to peace until we look back on our lives. Our lives represent our own personal evolutions.

The following list of the phases of my life exemplifies how lives might be seen as unfolding in phases, one phase evolving into another.

- **Childhood:** As a child, I knew I wanted to be something or do something important and worthwhile, something involving service. I carried a lot of guilt, sorrow, and shame, but I didn't know why.
- **Maturation:** As I matured, I began seeking answers to the "What makes me happy?" question. I acquired the things I thought would make me happy—a husband, a career (or two), a child (or two), a home, a better home, then a better home, a car, friends, lots of books ... you get the gist.
- **Adulthood:** As an adult, I had more and more achievements with more and more responsibilities while I became more and more anxious and depressed. I still wanted to make a difference. I still wanted to be happy. I *knew* underneath all that depression was a person who wanted to be loving, caring, and passionate about life. On the outside, my life looked like the perfect American dream, so where was the disconnection?
- **Internal shift:** It became obvious to me that the problem was not outside me, so I started looking internally. I was the common denominator regarding the problems in my life. I was also the solution.
- **Realization:** What startled me was how much I really, really hated myself. A lifetime of self-deprecation had taken a toll. The guilt was deep and ugly. Fear and anxiety were ever present. I continued asking myself, "Why was I so fearful? Where did the guilt come from? How do I fix it?"
- **Religion:** I had been in organized religion my whole life, so I knew that contributed to the guilt issue. Therefore, I began looking other places for spirituality and peace.
- **Law of attraction:** Looking in depth at the law of attraction (LOA) taught me that I did have the ability to change my beliefs. I could take charge of my state of mind. It also taught me how interconnected all of life is. I didn't see much change in my outward life because of the

LOA, but I did get the sense that it has a deep internal meaning and there is more going on in life than we can physically see. Even deeply studying the LOA, as I had studied organized religion, did not ease my internal suffering. I had a longing for peace that was not abated by trying to think positively or control my external circumstances.

- **Near-death experiences:** Study of near-death experiences (NDEs) led me to understand more about life and death and the fear of both. Anita Moorjani's book *Dying to Be Me* deeply resonated with me. Purpose in life made more sense. I felt more than ever that our purpose is to be ourselves as only we can be and that love is at the heart of everything. This book on NDEs addressed many ideas on death, and it helped me let go of a lot of fear.

- **Continued suffering:** By the time I was on two antidepressants and still having suicidal ideation, I was ready for something drastic. I thought, *There must be something better!* I surrendered to everything. I gave up control. I asked life for answers I could understand.

- ***A Course in Miracles*:** This was the response to my earnest and sincere prayer for an answer I could understand for my current state of mind. I committed to this self-study course, and it was the worst and best thing that ever happened to me. This book focuses on retraining the mind to forgiveness thinking. It released me from my attachments to stories and anger and individuality. My ego was strong, so unraveling and letting go of it was a very painful process. My ego was strong, but my willingness to be at peace was stronger.

- **Progress:** I removed one antidepressant. I made the choice for peace to be a conscious entity in my life. Peace must be practiced. A life of conditioned responses takes time to unravel. Everything that happens in my life is an opportunity to choose peace. Daily, I was presented with bad drivers, stubborn children, empty gas tanks, dirty clothes, and bills. I realized they are my chance to get free. The question was always "How important is my peace?" Then, I removed another antidepressant. Over a year later, I haven't added them back. I believe they can do a great deal of good when you need them. But I have passed through that phase—at least for now.

Some days, I fail at moving forward, learning, and growing. It feels like too much effort. I get exhausted with the effort of living productively. But I now know how to forgive. That alone makes it easier to start again and keep moving forward to do the next best thing for me. Each day, I get better and better at it. I should have a PhD in spiritual studies, but the goal isn't a degree; it is peace. It is hard to explain how someone who has had lofty, achievable, time-limited goals all her life can now have only one goal. That goal has no time frame, but is still lofty and achievable. Finding peace for the purpose of being love in the world is the most important thing I have ever done. Why? Because it affects everyone and everything in my life. This isn't just about me. I want my kids to see someone who is completely at peace. It isn't enough to talk about it. It must be demonstrated. It is the most unselfish selfish thing I have ever attempted.

Phases Inquiry

1. When you look back on your life, how has it evolved? Has it evolved in phases? What are they?

2. How have you forced things? How have you surrendered? How has this affected your life?

3. Do you experience inner peace? If not, what might be blocking it?

4.

Notes

_____

_____

_____

_____

_____

_____

_____

_____

_____

_____

_____

_____

_____

_____

_____

_____

_____

_____

_____

_____

10

Religion

There are many paths to God. Some of them lead you through religion and religious practices. In my personal experience of growing up Catholic, I was profoundly committed to the practice to the point that I went on a yearlong retreat for teens. I profoundly committed to the religion until I realized it was not serving me in finding either peace or God. I intend no judgment in that. Catholicism works for many good people—just not me. I then found the Episcopal Church, which is often described as "Catholic light" or "Catholic without the guilt." I found this to be true for the most part. I enjoyed the music, the ritual, and the ability to ask questions in an open forum. Yet it, too, was part of my path, not the whole path. I have attended Methodist, Quaker, and Baptist services. I have done yoga, tai chi, and meditation. They have all added to the information I use to make the next step on my path.

This is not going to be a religion bashing, although I have come to a point, at least for now, where participating in formalized religion is not for me. This was brought home for me when I attended a nondenominational church in our area this week. It is one of the largest churches in the area and is steadily growing. A young woman who drank, did drugs, and slept around while she was in high school was giving a lecture. In her story, she said she was saved from that kind of life when she found God, and she had loving parents who supported her. She now has a loving husband, a beautiful child, and another on the way. Hers is a story of personal redemption. I personally found her to be authentic and well meaning. She was brave in taking responsibility to change her life.

But I wanted to take issue with something in her comments. There is one thing that I feel is fundamentally askew with what is happening at that church and many other churches. She said, "Many of you are waiting until you are good enough for God. You'll never be good enough for God, but He says, 'Come to Me anyway.'" There were heads nodding all over the place; it was packed in there. A Christian rock band was literally singing about how sinful we are and how Jesus saved us. But I think we'll never be truly saved as Jesus intended if we believe this statement. It cannot be true, and I will tell you why.

It struck me then and there what Jesus had tried to tell us. God has never said to us that we will never be good enough. God says that we have always been good enough because we are made in His image. We cannot be from the Great Creator and be crap. Either we are from God or we are not. If we are from and of God, then we must be, at the heart and soul of us, great. This is what we have forgotten. Jesus remembered this, then taught us that we are not bodies but living souls of love and grace and that we return to that state and are forever safe and loved by God, or whatever you believe the Creator to be.

I wanted to embrace all these suffering souls around me and scream, "You are not bad! You are not sinful! You are not shameful!" When you remember you are of the Creator, of love, then that is what you act like. When you believe you are bad and sinful and shameful, then that is how you act. We must get the order right for God to truly work miracles in us and in religion. We must remember that we are made in God's image, not God in ours. I love this quote by the French philosopher Voltaire: "God made us in His image, and then we returned the favor." God is not judgmental, vengeful, or angry because God has not forgotten that He is love.

Religion Inquiry

1. What are you looking for in a spiritual path or religion? Are you finding it?

2. How do you perceive God, religion, and spirituality the same as or differently than you did five years ago? Ten years ago? Twenty years ago? Are you open to continuing to evolve?

3. Do you feel "good enough" for God?

4.

Notes

_____

_____

_____

_____

_____

_____

_____

_____

_____

_____

_____

_____

_____

_____

_____

_____

_____

_____

_____

Light Switch

The longing—or "yearning," as Gangaji calls it—has been with me for as long as I can remember. In the last ten years, I have done a lot of spiritual searching and growing. I have had the sense that I am in the dark, feeling my way along the wall, searching for a light switch. Once I find that light switch, I will flip the switch and flood the room with light. Turns out my switch is a dimmer.

Through listening to *Waking Up*, the inspirational series of interviews Tami Simon, publisher of Sounds True, did with current spiritual teachers, I found out that it is not unusual to have a journey of spiritual enlightenment. Although gurus might have an immediate and profound moment of awakening, most people evolve along a path of awakening. They, too, have a dimmer switch. This process is just as valid and profound as the quick flip of the switch.

To me, this is frustrating. I want to flip the switch and see the light. But apparently, part of my awakening process is to learn patience. I have also found that the last step from the dark to the light is not mine to make. I have every reason to believe this will happen for me, and for everyone, but the time of that occurrence is not up to me. My job is to work on undoing the blocks to peace; maintaining my openness to the way of my path, even though I often do not know the next step on it; keeping the faith that everything is for my good; and relying on the promise that love is truly the essence of life. The rest is up to life, or whatever you deem the Higher Source to be. "Let there be light!" is a prayer I still frequently say, but I am making peace with an increasingly warming glow. Dimmers eventually reveal the whole range of light possibilities. Maybe the process is meant to ensure that the light is not so bright as to blind. Maybe I am not so much increasing my light as decreasing my dark. Regardless, I seek illumination. I am willing to turn the dimmer switch dial, even if ever so slowly.

Light Switch Inquiry

1. How do you understand the metaphor of light? Do you have a dimmer switch?

2. How is your light shining? How do you nurture your light?

3. How do you feel about your personal spiritual development? How do you feel about the pace?

4.

Notes

_____

_____

_____

_____

_____

_____

_____

_____

_____

_____

_____

_____

_____

_____

_____

_____

_____

_____

_____

12

Intention

Once, outside a convenience store, I gave a couple of dollars to a man asking for money. Moments later, a woman whipped her car up next to me and shouted, "You know he's just going across the street to that other convenience store to buy beer or drugs or something!" Then, before I could respond, she whipped out of the parking lot and sped away. I marveled at this. She berated my giving the man money based on what she thought his intent was. How did she know he wasn't buying food or cigarettes? Either of those things may have brought him just as much comfort as beer. Why did it even matter to her what he bought? He was obviously walking, so it wasn't like he was going to drink and drive. Why begrudge him anything? And why was she so worried about his intention while completely dismissing mine?

It reminded me of another incident years earlier when my brother and I saw a man in an old van begging for money around Christmas. It was pretty cold for Mississippi, so we went out of our way to get hot coffee and biscuits to bring to him. As we drove up beside him, he got out of the van. He walked up, grabbed the food, turned around, and got back in his van with not a single word to us. Gratitude was not in his makeup. We learned a lot about our intention versus another's that day. It was likely he just wanted money. Ah, got it now. Yet he could have also been embarrassed. I have no way of knowing. It doesn't matter anyway. His reaction in no way changed our intent in giving.

Both these incidences highlight how an intention—in this case, the intention to give—is separate from a response. I have thought about these instances a lot over the years, and I have come to understand that a true and worthy intention does not depend on a perceived response or outcome. I have asked myself whether I should stop giving if someone observing the action is unhappy or if I should stop giving because the recipient may be ungrateful. This has pointed me back to my initial motives. Do I give only to get, or is the gift in the giving itself? The reward is the opportunity to offer myself, my money, and my resources. In my heart, I know that once I freely give something, I must freely release it. It is no longer mine to hold or direct or judge. But it can be judged by others, apparently. In each of these cases of giving, I didn't expect a certain reaction; but in each case, I intended to honestly help another human being.

In both these instances, once the food or money left my hands, it was no longer mine. It was theirs. They could do whatever they wanted with it. How freely is something given if it is burdened with conditions? How am I to know what a person really needs in each moment? That was their choice. My choice had already been fulfilled.

Our experiences in life depend on our expectations and our intent. I intend to find comfortable ways for me to give where there are organic opportunities for someone to receive. I will continue to strive to avoid ownership of what I give and therefore have no stake in the outcome. And so life will continue to find ways to receive what I am offering, whether through a homeless man, through my art, or through a hug—whatever. The point is that I intend to do what I am inspired to do and follow it through. But what I have come to understand is that once an intention is out there, it can be interpreted and responded to differently due to other people's intentions and agendas. That need not affect me. My intentions are a personal affair.

My overall intention is to interact honestly in the world. That's it. What I hope goes with the stuff I give, as I hand it to another, is my most sincere internal blessing as a giver to a receiver. Whether the receiver registers that consciously or unconsciously or not at all matters not. The intention is there. It is enough.

Intention Inquiry

1. What are your intentions about giving?

2. How do you respond, internally and externally, to other people's reactions to your actions?

3. Do you have expectations for those receiving resources or gifts from you?

4.

Notes

_____

_____

_____

_____

_____

_____

_____

_____

_____

_____

_____

_____

_____

_____

_____

_____

_____

_____

_____

_____

13

Love by Choice

"Mom, all the animals like you best," my son says as my daughter is nodding behind him.

"Of course they do," I agree, "because I feed, water, and pet them."

Relationships take time and attention. All solid, meaningful relationships require that kind of investment. For pets, it isn't just a matter of putting food in a bowl. The food needs to be nutritious, balanced, tasteful, and just the right amount. As I write this, I have a nine-pound poodle resting in her bed beside me and a thirteen-pound cat on my desk pushing at the computer, stepping on the keys. I didn't put them there; they came of their own free will, of their own volition.

As I lie down in bed at night, I am amazed that there is a dog at my feet, a cat above my head, and another at my side. Sometimes, when I wake in the night, I can't turn over because they are so close. They have to be touching me. I am so used to it now that when I travel, I can barely get to sleep because there aren't furry somebodies snuggling against me. What most amazes me is that they are there because they *want* to be there. My heart swells with gratitude as I think about it. They have increased my capacity to love.

You see, I try my very best not to make them sit with me or accompany me anywhere. They always have a choice of where they want to be when there are people at home. I do not force them to sit in my lap, on my desk, on my bed, on the chair, or on the porch. So when they willingly knead my stomach or rest their heads on my leg, it thrills me beyond words because they have chosen to be there.

They give me a gift every time they choose to be with me. They give me the gift of themselves. They can only be what they are. There is no analyzing or second-guessing; there is no underhanded agenda. They are real and honest in their actions. You cannot make an animal love you. It does, or it doesn't.

I never presume that they think like humans. In fact, I am eternally grateful that they don't. I love them, and they love me—simple as that. There is no need for rationalization or supposition. It isn't the kind of love you think about. Love is. You know it. That is enough.

Looking at my two-legged children, I realize that I have the same opportunity to let go of the outcome. They choose to be with me or not. They are free to leave; they are free to come home. I want to know that they are there by choice. When my daughter comes in at night and tells me about her social activities, and when my son comes out of his room to tell me about his high score in gaming, they are choosing to share their lives with me. The very best I can do is to be ever present to them, appreciate them, and know the love.

Love by Choice Inquiry

1. How do you recognize love in your life?

2. What makes your heart swell with love or gratitude?

3. Are all the beings in your life free to come and go?

4.

Notes

_____

_____

_____

_____

_____

_____

_____

_____

_____

_____

_____

_____

_____

_____

_____

_____

_____

_____

_____

14

Being Seen

To teach is to demonstrate.

—A Course in Miracles

Throughout my whole academic career, I tried to be an exemplary student. My parents were both teachers, so education was a priority in our home. I wanted to please my teachers as well as my parents, so I worked hard at my studies. I wasn't valedictorian material, but I managed to graduate in the top half of my high school class. Even so, when awards day rolled around senior year, I didn't receive anything noteworthy. I could not understand why I was heartbroken when we left the gym. Awards and recognition have never really meant that much to me. In fact, I have always been very shy, so I've always dreaded being called out in front of everyone. So, why did it hurt so much?

On the way back to class, one of my teachers stopped me in the schoolyard. He said, "Brigid, every year, there seems to be a really good student that gets left out of being recognized. This year, that student was you." This was just between us; no one else heard what he said. I was stunned, and so very grateful. In that one moment, he made all that hard work worth it.

I have come to understand why that was the case. It was the simple fact that he had seen me. I wasn't just a number or another student passing before him who he would soon forget. He saw how hard I had tried, and he took the time to tell me that my effort had not gone unnoticed.

I will never forget that moment, although he most likely has. He taught me how much it means to really see someone. That has been one of the most important lessons of my life. I have remembered it throughout my life and tried to apply it as best as I can to everyone I meet. One of the most important things I learned from a teacher did not happen in the classroom, and it didn't come from a textbook or school curriculum. It happened my senior year right before graduation, in a schoolyard, and took about thirty seconds of his time. That teacher demonstrated that it doesn't take much time or effort to positively influence, even change, a person's life.

Being Seen Inquiry

1. Who in your life really sees you?

2. Who do you make an effort to really notice? How have you, or might you, let them know?

3. Who might need you to really see them? What happens in you when you deliberately see someone?

4.

Notes

_____

_____

_____

_____

_____

_____

_____

_____

_____

_____

_____

_____

_____

_____

_____

_____

_____

_____

_____

_____

True Love

I am.

Love is.

I am what love is.

It seems so cliché to talk about what love is. Its presence and absence seem to be all around us in various forms and to various degrees. I love my children, my pets, my parents, my siblings, and my friends. But that is easily said and done. It feels wonderful when love is present, and I feel bereft when I withhold it from someone or feel that it is being withheld from me. The big question is "What is true love?"

Can I love my neighbor? My grocer? My enemy? Can I love terrorists, politicians, and drunk drivers? Can I love myself?

Can I see everyone and everything without judgment? Can I understand that life sees me that way? Can I be as unrelenting in my forgiveness and patience and peace as I have been in my judgment and condemnation?

I hope so, because I truly know that if I don't try, I will not know what true love is.

True Love Inquiry

    1.   What is true love to you?

    2.   How has love been conditional or unconditional in your life?

    3.   Have you loved unconditionally? Have you been loved unconditionally?

    4.   Are true love and unconditional love the same thing to you?

    5.

Notes

_____

_____

_____

_____

_____

_____

_____

_____

_____

_____

_____

_____

_____

_____

_____

_____

_____

_____

16

Good or Bad

When people see some things as beautiful, other things become ugly. When people see some things as good, other things become bad.

—*Tao Te Ching* (translated by Stephen Mitchell)

"It's definitely a copperhead," my husband said as he examined the small snake curled up in the middle of the road. Luckily, it was only about eight inches long. We were walking in our neighborhood at roughly 9:00 p.m., so we almost missed seeing it. My husband's first instinct was to kill it—which is a very common reaction by most people in my experience.

But I have always seen snakes differently than most do. That is in part because my mother is a biologist. When my siblings and I were young, she would bring nonpoisonous snakes into the house for us to hold and observe. I learned early about which ones are dangerous and which ones are beneficial. And my medical training encourages me to identify snakes as symbols of healing. They can be found wrapped around both the caduceus in human medicine and the staff of Asclepius in veterinary medicine. These medical symbols look similar, but the human caduceus has two snakes wrapped around a staff whereas the veterinary staff has one.

Of course, copperheads are dangerous snakes. But this one was taking advantage of the quiet night to lie in the middle of the warm road. It did not move at all as we passed by it. "I am concerned it may bite someone," my husband was saying. "It could have bitten us."

But I was thinking back to the discussion my meditation group had had just that morning. It centered on the quote in chapter 2 of the *Tao Te Ching* that says when we judge something as good, other things become bad. I looked at the little snake in the road as it was just being there—just being what it was—no more, no less. So I asked my husband to please leave it alone. "But it could bite someone," he repeated.

I asked my husband to consider that the snake was just doing what snakes do. It didn't try to bite us when we passed it by or when we turned around and examined it with a flashlight. It just continued being there. To make a life-and-death decision now about what the snake might do in the future would make the snake bad when it was just lying there. We could not know what the snake was going to do. To say that the snake might bite would be the same as looking at my teenager and saying that she might drink or smoke, or looking at my husband and saying he might cheat on me. We all have possibilities and choices.

The little snake in the road gave me an opportunity to look at my current way of judging good versus bad. It allowed me to reevaluate my concepts of good and bad and the way I label and judge my world. Snakes shed their skin, so we can shed the old for the new. How lovely that an eight-inch poisonous baby snake represented its species so well just by being, and in doing so lived up to its lofty status as a symbol of healing.

Good or Bad Inquiry

1. What have you seen with fear that you could see as a symbol of love or healing?

2. What judgments can you release about yourself? Others?

3. When was your last big shift in perspective? Did it come from something big or small?

4.

Notes

_____

_____

_____

_____

_____

_____

_____

_____

_____

_____

_____

_____

_____

_____

_____

_____

_____

_____

_____

Sadness and a Good Life

My life has been blessed with situational perfection. In other words, I was raised by two parents (well, mostly) and my mother's parents; we did not have much money, but we always had food on the table and clothes on our backs (not designer, often homemade); we were healthy (at least physically); and we got good educations and subsequently got good jobs and careers. I fell in love in college, bought a house, had two children, bought a bigger house, changed jobs, won a couple of awards, yada yada yada. In other words, there is absolutely no person or situation to blame for the depression and anxiety I have had almost my entire life. It is wonderful that I haven't lost a child to an illness (my biggest nightmare) or my spouse to cancer because I could see me easily blaming such conditions outside myself for my sorry mental state.

If you knew me, you would never, ever guess that I have spent a good part of my life depressed or anxious. In public, I am typically upbeat, engaging, and supportive. Many times in private, I have wanted to just curl up in the fetal position, pull my covers over my head, and disappear. Again, I have had a blessed life in spite of the depression and anxiety. Realization of the fact that you have had a blessed life does not change depression. It makes you feel guilty for not being able to be fully grateful for it. I understood that I was not depressed because I had a bad life in the same way I was not happy because I had a good life.

In veterinary school, my stress was so overwhelming that I had night terrors. I did try to reach out for help, but the campus physician recommended I do more praying. Medical school obviously must have been easier than veterinary school if he even remotely thought I wasn't already doing that!

Taking full responsibility for my state of mental affairs, I got on antidepressants. I was on two different antidepressants when I fully surrendered to the force higher than myself. By that point, I just knew there had to be a better way than medicating my way through each day. Please don't get me wrong. I am all for medication as needed. But adding drugs had not brought me relief. I had begun having suicidal ideation. There had to be another way, or at least a complementary way.

And so I began the spiritual journey I am currently on. I surrendered with the understanding that I would do my part by not second-guessing the process, by being completely and totally honest, by being vulnerable, and by not shying away from pain. I knew total surrender could change my entire life.

My external conditions were proof to me that my depression was not due to something outside myself. Nothing external had to change for my depression and anxiety to ease; at this point in my journey, I haven't had to move and haven't lost my job, but I have lost lots of things I didn't want—including two antidepressants. Many instances may call for external change; and it may yet be required for me. But I know it to be true now that my depression has ultimately been a blessing for me because it indicated something was wrong and there had to be a better way for me to experience life.

Sadness and a Good Life Inquiry

1. How is your inner life speaking to you?

2. How have your hardships held blessings for your life?

3. In what ways do you mask your pain? Why? What is your pain trying to tell you?

4.

Notes

_____

_____

_____

_____

_____

_____

_____

_____

_____

_____

_____

_____

_____

_____

_____

_____

_____

_____

_____

_____

18

Alive

What a gift kids are! What gifts they give.

For instance, my son had one of the best summer vacations of his life when he was six years old. He got to spend lots of time swimming, riding bikes, sleeping in late, and playing his video games. The most fun was going on field trips with his sister and his YaYa (Greek for "grandmother").

They went on field trips to the Insect Museum, the Natural Science Museum, the New Orleans Zoo, and the planetarium. The best trip of all was to SeaWorld in Orlando, Florida. My son loves all animals, but he is really fond of aquatic animals. He was excited to see Shamu, the killer whale. He and his cousin sat in the front row of the killer whale show so they could see Shamu up close. Shamu swam near them and splashed a huge wave over them, just as they had hoped. They were soaked from head to toe. As soon as Shamu splashed them, my son jumped up and yelled out, in front of the whole crowd, "Yes!" Of course, everyone around him got a big kick out of the joy coming from this little boy.

As they were walking out of the show, YaYa asked him how he felt. My son said in his most excited voice, his face all shiny and lit up, "I feel alive!"

In those three words, he reminded us how the simple things in life can give us the most satisfaction and touch the place where pure joy is alive in us. His joy was extremely evident and infectious to all around him. I don't know why we, as adults, often get caught up in obsessing about the past or future and forget how to make the most of these simple *now* moments. Leave it to kids to bring us back to what truly matters in all of us.

Alive Inquiry

1. What lights you up with joy from the inside out?

2. What makes you feel alive? When do you feel the most alive?

3.

Notes

_____

_____

_____

_____

_____

_____

_____

_____

_____

_____

_____

_____

_____

_____

_____

_____

_____

_____

_____

_____

19

Comfort

When I can't find love,
There is a place that comforts me.
Her soft body curled against my leg,
I touch her softly,
Offering my heart for healing.
Purring begins as
Love floods in.

When I can't find love,
There is a place that comforts me.
His wet nose in the crook of my arm,
I gaze into the depths of grace.
We lean together.
I am awed as
Love comes rushing in.

Hazel was a gray tortoiseshell cat we got from a local veterinarian as a rescue. She was as close to an angel on earth as I have ever met. What a peaceful presence. Eckhart Tolle once said, "I have lived with many Zen masters—all of them cats." I get that. In fact, one of those cats is sitting on my desk next to my computer as I type. Well, this cat happens to be Zen-ish.

But our cat Hazel was as Zen as they come. Her presence alone was comforting. For instance, when my toddler daughter went to her room crying, Hazel would paw at the door to be let in. I would often find Hazel leaning against her legs, or curled against her body, just being there. As a mother, I couldn't have asked for a better friend for my daughter. As a seeker, I couldn't have found a better teacher.

So often we are left alone with the intensity of our irrational pain. A true friend is one who sits with you, offering comfort as you recover. True friends don't tell you it will be all right, give you counsel, or say to put on your big-girl panties or to buck up. They sit with you while you cry your eyes out. They extend their peace, their grace, and their simple presence. They let you know you aren't alone.

God, I miss that cat. As I think of Hazel, I can feel her presence. Love comes rushing in.

Comfort Inquiry

1. What is a wholesome source of comfort for you?

2. Who have you offered comfort to?

3. What words or actions give you the most comfort?

4. Can you trust enough or are you willing to be vulnerable to allow someone to comfort you?

5.

Notes

_____

_____

_____

_____

_____

_____

_____

_____

_____

_____

_____

_____

_____

_____

_____

_____

_____

_____

_____

_____

Left Turns

I have found that simple, everyday activities experienced with awareness and deliberateness can affect all parts of life. Performing left turns while driving is an example. When I was just beginning to drive, I overheard my uncle tell someone that he tries to make only right-hand turns. He explained how he would go out of his way to make a block so that he would end up at a light with an arrow, or he would make numerous rights until he ended up headed in his desired direction. This was much safer than turning left across oncoming traffic. Rights were easier. Rights were safer.

Yes, it is much safer to take safe rights until you find a safe left. But then comes the time you just have to take a left turn. For instance, most days, I take my son to school and must go through the car line with the myriad other makes and models of family transportation. It is all right turns on the way in. There is one turn going out that is particularly trying. Even though it is a small town, the road is a major thoroughfare with cars turning both left and right into the school, and a stop sign suspending traffic so that it blocks the entrance. Into the fray, a left turn is required. This left turn causes a particular stab of anxiety because it isn't safe and you must be patient. I could go around, and have done so, but it is a great deal out of the way.

One day after pondering the pros and cons of taking this particular left turn, I decided to ask for spiritual help. Having dropped off my son, I started back the way I had come with the full intention of taking that left turn. Before I got there, I asked life to clear my path so that I wouldn't get in a wreck or become unduly stressed with having to move into the heavy traffic. Somewhere inside me, there was a knowing of "I got this." That's it. I knew I was lined up with the assistance I needed. Then, I surrendered to it with total trust. Needless to say, it was easy peasy lemon squeezy. And I have been asking for help ever since. Sometimes, I sit there for a few minutes. But no matter what, I am able to make that left turn safely without anxiety. Sometimes, it is completely clear. Sometimes, I have to gun it, but always, I am safe and feel safe.

Now, whenever I approach something that I must do and I am filled with anxiety about getting it done, I do a spiritual left turn. This has become the way of my spiritual path. I doubt that traffic is really that different just for me. The fact is that my mind is now different about taking left turns.

Since then, I have had a number of spiritual left turns. And every time, I am amazed that they just work. They are part of the everyday fabric of my life and available to me at all times. They remind me that if I have faith, life will show me it is working on my behalf with even everyday needs.

I still prefer right turns, but left turns are necessary in my life, and I appreciate them. A right turn doesn't remind me that I am ultimately taken care of in this place where I am now. It is a left turn that keeps me on my toes, makes me come back to awareness, and makes me get beyond myself by asking for help in changing my way of dealing with the world. These left turns have included the death of a parent, my children leaving home, and my divorce. The little everyday things are what make a difference for all the other everyday things that make up the quality of the experience of life.

Left Turns Inquiry

1. What are your personal left turns?

2. How might you play or cocreate with life?

3. What situations make you feel unsafe, and what help do you need to handle them with ease?

4.

Notes

_____

_____

_____

_____

_____

_____

_____

_____

_____

_____

_____

_____

_____

_____

_____

_____

_____

_____

_____

_____

_____

More Than a Body

You wouldn't get the impression from this essay's title that this is about the most profound spiritual experience of my life. You wouldn't get that this is about life, not death. But this is absolutely about how a death changed my perception of life.

When I was a freshman in college, I went to a small private university in Eastern Ohio. My major was mental health studies. One of the class's elective field trips was to the medical examiner's office in Philadelphia, Pennsylvania. A court officer met us and prepped us with information about the office, including the fact that every unexplained death must be autopsied. He explained that downstairs, there was the body of a young woman who had apparently drowned in the Allegheny River.

He took us into the room where she was being autopsied. She had already been opened from her neck to her pubis. Her organs had been taken out, and the medical examiner's staff were in the process of weighing each one when we filed in. An incision had been made in a semicircle from one side of her head to the other, and her scalp had been peeled forward and was lying over her face. A circular incision with a notch had been made in her skull, and the skull cap had been removed so they could also remove the brain.

We moved to one side of the autopsy room so that we could observe the process. The court official explained what was going on. He realized it was a lot to take in, explaining how it had taken the staff who worked there time to get used to it as well. But since it had become so familiar, they could now come and go while eating lunch if they needed to.

During this explanation, he gave me a visual I will never forget. He said, "Think of her body as a house versus a home. A home is a place where people live. A house is just an empty building. This body is a house now; there isn't anyone living there any longer."

When they folded the top of her head back, it was like her face popped up. It was only then that I got a sense of who she had been as a real, live person. The sudden view of her face gave her a persona. I realized that as good as medical science is, the pieces of her couldn't just be put back together to bring her back to life. In that moment, I understood that something *other than* the brain or body composed the essence of this woman. What had been truly alive and real about her was no longer there. Well, it was no longer in that body.

I have thought a lot about that over the last twenty-five years. I heard a saying that we are not physical beings having spiritual experiences; we are spiritual beings having physical experiences. That resonated with me as I thought back to that day in autopsy. Based on this, I believe the essence of life lies not in our bodies but in our spirits. Our spirits are our true and eternal lives. One's spirit is the self one longs to experience. That is the self that is without the descriptors of our parents, the evaluations of our teachers or bosses, the recollections of our past, or the shapes of our bodies. It cannot be judged or defined or threatened. It is freedom itself. Therefore, it stands to reason that by being true to our spirits, we can allow them to be expressed. That expression is the ultimate experience of this life.

More Than a Body Inquiry

1. How is your spirit expressing itself in this physical experience?

2. Are you willing to consider that your body is not who you are? If so, as you consider yourself as a spiritual entity, how do your feelings about yourself change?

3.

Notes

_____

_____

_____

_____

_____

_____

_____

_____

_____

_____

_____

_____

_____

_____

_____

_____

_____

_____

_____

_____

Freedom

Oliver was young when he came to live with us. His previous owners had gotten him declawed and had then put him outside when they decided to get a divorce. We thought it was anger or cruelty that made the man put his former wife's cat outside. But it was fairly evident to us from the very beginning that Oliver longed to be outside. He loved looking out the window or the glass door at birds and lizards. His longing became an obsession, as he would stand by the door and mournfully meow and whine. The longing became stronger than the risk. At first, we ignored his plaintive wailing by the door. Then, we could bear it no longer when his whining became incessant.

It started with us letting him out a bit at a time while watching him. He was so happy that we started extending the time frame that he could roam. He would come back a couple of hours later. Then he would come back in the morning. Then one morning, he did not come back. We looked for him for weeks, but we knew he was what he really wanted to be—free. Some cats never glance at a door or through a window. They are content to meditate in a ray of sunshine as it falls across a comforter. Oliver needed to be in the shadows and the light. He could not be completely himself looking out from the inside. He knew what he wanted and was willing to risk it all.

Many will say that I made the wrong decision letting him outside, knowing he was declawed. But I look at my own life and ask if I should quit longing for what I really want and just play it safe. The news media, education, LISTSERVs, and so on have left me declawed. But should I stop living because I am afraid for my safety? In my heart, I have learned to go outside, to take risks when it may not be safe, to write and let people read it, and to submit my art to journals or even just post it on Facebook.

So, I told Oliver that I supported him; that life is about quality, not quantity; that I understood his longing; and that he was free to go and come back. The door is still open to him. The window is open as well, but now, it is me glancing out to catch a glimpse of him in the sun.

Freedom Inquiry

1. How do you play it safe?

2. What do you long for that you repress? What would happen if you didn't repress it?

3. What habits, responsibilities, or obligations keep you from adventures you long for?

4.

Notes

_____

_____

_____

_____

_____

_____

_____

_____

_____

_____

_____

_____

_____

_____

_____

_____

_____

_____

_____

_____

Feeding the Good Wolf

I am a meditation fail. Yesterday, when I was meditating in our weekly group meeting, the thought *What if my eyes were on my butt?* popped into my head. Strangely enough, this was indeed a spiritual question. Most spiritual leaders encourage you to drop into your center, or get out of your head, to find your balance and your centeredness. Would we associate ourselves with our heads so much if most of our senses weren't so close to our brains? If our eyes were on our butts, would we have a completely different perspective of the world? If our eyes were located at our center of gravity, wouldn't we naturally have a greater sense of balance? Maybe this thought comes from considering so many species and how they look at the world differently; regardless, it is interesting to consider.

The meditation reading used that day was from Adyashanti's *The Way of Liberation*: "In True Meditation the emphasis is on being awareness—not on being aware of objects but on resting as *conscious being* itself. In meditation you are not trying to change your experience; you are changing your *relationship to* your experience." Obviously, my fail was at the "resting" part. But I was certainly considering changing my relationship to my experience.

My understanding was that it wasn't about something outside me that made up my experience. My relationship to my external experience is solely based on my internal experience—my relationship to myself, to my being. Many times, this relationship is purely unconscious, which means I have not taken responsibility for my inner state.

My mind is in an almost-constant state of activity. I was trained to think. That is why meditation is so useful. It is kind and gentle mind training. For me, it is often frustrating because I have to deal with the incessant chatter of thought. I have *finally* gotten to the point where I can watch my thoughts without trying to resist or stop them. I have *finally* gotten to the point where I can distinguish my being from my thoughts. Up to this point in my life, I was what I thought about. Oh my God, what a relief not to believe everything I think about!

It reminds me of the Cherokee legend about the two wolves. An old Cherokee was teaching his grandson about life. "A fight is going on inside me," he said to the boy. "It is a terrible fight, and it is between two wolves. One is evil—he is anger, envy, sorrow, regret, greed, arrogance, self-pity, guilt, resentment, inferiority, lies, false pride, superiority, and ego." He continued, "The other is good—he is joy, peace, love, hope, serenity, humility, kindness, benevolence, empathy, generosity, truth, compassion, and faith. The same fight is going on inside you—and inside every other person too."

The grandson thought about it for a minute and then asked his grandfather, "Which wolf will win?"

The old Cherokee simply replied, "The one you feed."

Meditating, focusing on being, not believing my thinking, and changing my perspective all feed the good wolf.

Feeding the Good Wolf Inquiry

1. What practices have given you a greater sense of just being?

2. Which wolf are you feeding?

3. How often do you believe your thoughts and emotions are realities?

4.

Notes

_____

_____

_____

_____

_____

_____

_____

_____

_____

_____

_____

_____

_____

_____

_____

_____

_____

_____

_____

_____

24

Learning by Example

Have you ever noticed that some of the most important, meaningful lessons you ever learn are given to you by people or events that aren't trying to "teach" you anything? Coming to mind right now are two very different people who taught me two very different lessons.

When I first encountered Dr. Mary, I was a very new public health nurse. My territory covered nine counties. One day, I went to the office after traveling the area and found a note to call Dr. Mary. At the time, she was a consulting physician for the tuberculosis control unit. Her office was located in the capitol, roughly two hundred miles south of my location.

As a nurse, I had been taught to be both respectful and differential to physicians. Being young and relatively new—translate that as *intimidated*—I called her back and said something to the effect of "Hello, Dr. Currier. This is Brigid returning your call." The very first thing she said was "Please call me Mary."

Seems simple enough, right? People give their names to each other every day. But physicians aren't regular people; most people think of them as the closest thing to God. It was like having God say, "Just call me G."

I have known Mary for almost thirty years now, and I have never known her to be anything but available, personal, and brilliant. She has been completely dedicated to bettering the health and welfare of the public her entire career. I have admired her profoundly, without intimidation, that entire time. She taught me that a degree does not equal respect. She showed me by example how to see everyone's worth equally and to respect our different contributions. In my career, I have tried very hard to emulate that.

Now, Mr. Willie was the head of building services when I was in veterinary school. A distinguished-looking man with an extremely likable personality, he would enter through the end doors of our study/laboratory room and yell, "Doc-tors!" He'd look at all of us freshmen and just smile broadly. I mean he would *really* look at us and smile, repeating, "Doc-tors!" You know, he was the first person to make it real for me. We had gotten the prerequisites, filled out the lengthy application, passed the interview, and gotten the lab coat. We were newbie freshmen overwhelmed by the responsibility, wondering what the hell we had gotten ourselves into, then "Doc-tors!" Thank God for Mr. Willie. He read our future, and we believed! Amen!

Mr. Willie had every key to every nook and cranny in that building. He knew secrets. He knew our deepest secret. In the beginning, we needed to see ourselves at the end, having made our dream a reality. Veterinary school did not just teach us about medicine; it taught us about character, and about being part of a noble profession. Mr. Willie is an indelible part of the profession for me. He made me what I am as surely as Mary did.

They both lived and influenced by example. Mary connected with people as partners, equal in ability and intent to do service, even if not equal in knowledge. Mr. Willie uplifted us and taught me to live my intention today. He also taught me that all of us have something to offer as we are now. He taught me how one person can do that for another in how we interact with others. As I write this, I feel this coming home to me again. In my experience, every single person you encounter has a gift to offer if you are open to receiving it. Some offer more than others, for sure. But if you aren't open to receiving these gifts, how will you ever know?

Learning by Example Inquiry

1. Who do you admire, and who have you known who has led or taught by positive example?

2. How have they affected your decisions? Your life?

3. What character traits do you most admire about yourself?

4.

Notes

_____

_____

_____

_____

_____

_____

_____

_____

_____

_____

_____

_____

_____

_____

_____

_____

_____

_____

25

Resistance to Assistance

There was a time in our lives when the first thing my husband would say when he woke up was "Shit!" He said it every morning for months! Oh, how I hated that. That is not the way I wanted to greet the world. Yet when I stood up from bed this morning, the first thing I said out loud was "Fuck!" Then I noticed my chest was hurting. Why don't I want to go to work or even breathe? There is nothing I am dreading; there is nothing wrong in my world other than the usual stuff—teenage kids, attempts to sell a house, bills. The pain just won't let up. Time to call someone.

ME: Mom! Lunch is on me.

There is nothing more therapeutic than sitting across from someone who gets you while you eat your way through chips and salsa—unless it also involves a pitcher of margaritas. At lunch, Mom asked some great questions. I was no help.

MOM (a.k.a. my personal therapist): What could you do right now that would give you some relief?

ME, *taking a long pause*: Run away. (*Takes another long pause.*) Nah, that would just set up an external diversion, and it wouldn't be worth hurting the family.

MOM: Okay. What skills from your childhood could you use now?

ME: I could suck my thumb, but I think that would cause a whole other type of discomfort. Not really looking to replace depression with shame.

MOM: Okay. How can you use what is going on for your good?

ME: Going to have to drink, I mean think, about that one. Thanks. Let's see. How can I use stubbornness and intensity to deal? Still thinking. Wait, I am thinking too much. Going to sit with it and see what happens.

So, my problem isn't solved. But I do feel heard and understood. A significant amount of the pressure in my chest has been relieved. Now, I may be able to relax enough to work this out on my own in spite of myself. Thank God for mothers, friends, confidants, and therapists (be they personal or professional).

Resistance to Assistance Inquiry

1. Are you able to reach out for help when you need it?

2. Where are you stubborn with yourself or others? How is it serving you?

3. Have you ever been resistant to assistance? Why?

4.

Notes

_____

_____

_____

_____

_____

_____

_____

_____

_____

_____

_____

_____

_____

_____

_____

_____

_____

_____

_____

26

Anguish

Anguish is a word you rarely hear, and it is not usually talked about except behind the closed doors of psychiatrists' offices and, possibly, showers. I have found anguish to be instrumental in the process of growing spiritually. It could very well be necessary for purging, as painful as it is. I have twice found myself curled in a ball on the shower floor, bawling my eyes out and calling out to God for help. No one had died; we hadn't lost all our money; and I hadn't lost a child, pet, or best friend. I was just coming undone. My ego was taking a hit. I didn't know who I was or which end was up. *Who am I without the story of myself? What do I do next? Why does it hurt to become nothing as I release stories of myself?*

Maybe growing doesn't have to hurt. Maybe my tears showed how tightly I had been hanging on to the past and how much I feared my future. *A Course in Miracles* promises that once you are free of your ego (the thought system of fear rather than the thought system of love and forgiveness), you will not miss it. I have found that to be true. But it is an ongoing process. Some people, like Eckhart Tolle and Byron Katie, are rid of their egos all at once. For most of us, it is a gradual process, like pulling off a Band-Aid very slowly.

So why even try to grow spiritually? Because deep in the heart of us, we long to live authentically, not through stories that we or other people have created. We long to know ourselves truly and thereby know others truly. Our stories keep us separated. Our authenticity unites us, removes our fear. It is the *something better* we know is out there. Living authentically means to live as our true selves, hearts wide-open, unafraid of other people or situations. It means to live each moment as it is, without the filter of the stories from our past.

Anguish is an emotional and deep-seated cleansing. I found that curling up in a ball squeezed out all the emotional toxins stored in my body while the water from the shower washed them away. I have never emerged from the "anguish shower" feeling refreshed. But I have emerged raw and renewed. I know where I am vulnerable, where my hurts have been hidden, and how I can surrender.

As I write, I can feel my heart and gut wrenching. I have learned that feeling and expressing pain safely is a healing process. Vulnerability is my strength, not my weakness. To be able to stand naked, literally and figuratively, in the face of my internal anguish is both humbling and empowering. I have washed the pain down the drain, so it does not wash over my family or my friends.

No longer afraid of anguish, I marvel at my depth of feeling. Can I express love more deeply now that I am no longer filled with so much pain? I don't look forward to anguish or plan anguish shower dates. But I don't fear them either. What we resist persists. So I now let anguish move through me to be washed away in warmth. Then I dry myself out and off and move on.

Note: Anguish can be overwhelming. If you find yourself in agony and unable to release it on your own, please reach out to a family member, friend, or professional counselor. I frequently find someone to talk to about these kinds of instances, and it helps tremendously.

Anguish Inquiry

1. How is anguish your ally?

2. Where might you need to become unstuck?

3. What have you learned from anguish?

4.

Notes

_____

_____

_____

_____

_____

_____

_____

_____

_____

_____

_____

_____

_____

_____

_____

_____

_____

_____

_____

27

Exuberance

One summer day many years ago, I went to visit a good friend who had a veterinary practice in town. I was still in nursing at the time and had not applied to veterinary school yet. In the animal clinic were some cages with all kinds of kittens in them. There were orange kittens, black kittens, striped kittens, and spotted kittens all living together in a bunch. Whenever someone would walk by, all the kittens would get up and meow. There was one little kitten who had on a blue collar with a bell. When I walked by the cage, the little kitten stepped on the heads of the other kittens as he reached his arm out as far as it would go. He'd swat the air trying to touch me. Every time he stepped on another kitten and reached out his arm, his bell would ring very loudly. I fell in love with him right then and there.

I went home and told my husband about the little kitten. Later that day, he surprised me by bringing the little kitten home with him. Although I was really surprised and happy, there was one problem. We already had a full-grown cat named Squirt. She instantly detested both him and his bell when the first thing he did was go running from one end of the house to the other. He kept sliding into the walls, turning around, running to the other end of the house, sliding into the wall, turning around, and then running to the end of the house. I couldn't help but think this might be the craziest cat I had ever seen. The bell on his collar kept going *ring, ring, ring, ring, ring, riiiiiing—ring, ring, ring, ring, ring, riiiiiing*, over and over again. I called my veterinarian friend to tell her that the cat might not be right in the head. Her opinion was that the cat was really, really, really happy to be out of the cage.

Temporarily mollified, I went to the store to get some cat litter and food for the little kitten. When I got home, the little kitten—whom we named Tibby for Sergeant Tibbs in *101 Dalmatians* (one of my favorite movies growing up—was sound asleep on the couch. I took that opportunity to remove the bell from his collar. It didn't help to take his bell off, though. Squirt never did learn to like Tibby. It didn't matter; Tibby settled in and grew into a delightful cat with plenty of character, eventually winning the dubious honor of "the funniest cat" in the local newspaper contest for sitting on the couch like a human complete with beer belly and TV remote by his side.

I think about that crazy kind of joy sometimes. What a gift freedom can be. I don't think I have ever displayed that kind of exuberance over anything. It should remind me of how fortunate I really am. I pray I don't have to lose something as precious as my freedom to remember how to exalt in gratitude, and how to be a little crazy with my joy.

Exuberance Inquiry

1. When have you felt exuberant? When have you allowed yourself to be embarrassingly joyful?

2. Do you allow yourself to be noticed in the world and uninhibitedly reach out for what you need or want?

3. Have you ever resented someone else's exuberance?

4.

Notes

_____

_____

_____

_____

_____

_____

_____

_____

_____

_____

_____

_____

_____

_____

_____

_____

_____

_____

_____

_____

Affirmation

Imagine that God gave you a most beautiful affirmation for your life today. And the affirmation is …

—Robert Holden

Happiness psychologist and inspirational speaker Robert Holden sends out daily messages by email and on Facebook. This quote is one that stimulated a lot of interesting inquiry for me.

The most fascinating thing was that, at first, I honestly couldn't answer it. Instead of being able to quickly and directly answer what beautiful affirmation I needed today, I found myself with more questions, such as "Do I need affirmation? What do I need affirmed? Would I affirm the right things?" *A Course in Miracles* talks about how we really don't know what makes us happy. This is because we don't know all the things that will ultimately inform our lives, so we may not know what is best for us. I like this because, rather than categorizing things as good or bad, I can trust that my life is unfolding as it should. This is what Byron Katie, author of *Loving What Is*, meant when she said, "Everything happens for us, not to us." With this in mind, I decided not to come up with an affirmation but to observe how my life was being affirmed, as I accepted what came up as being for me.

Two days later, I had an unusual and very specific example. My husband and I had been trying to sell our house for three years. For most of that time, we had rented it out. Our latest renters had indicated they wanted to buy the house. Yay! It was a bit of an emotional roller coaster, as house buying and selling usually are. My husband had offered them a great deal, but they backed out. Aw! They had come back to us with another offer; we settled on a price. Yay! The termite and home inspection got completed. Yay! However, the buyers made a request for us to pay for a termite treatment in addition to the home-inspection repairs. Aw! Up until that point, we had tried to make every concession we could. We did not feel comfortable paying for additional requests outside of the contract. Although we really wanted to sell the house, we wanted it to happen in a way that was fair to them and to us. We knew at every point that the deal might fall through.

Before we made the final arrangements for doing some of the repairs identified on the inspection report, and before the buyers knew we were uncomfortable with their additional request, the realtor contacted us to tell us that they had come back with an offer to remove their stipulation that fell outside the contract. Yay! This concession was completely out of character based on what we had experienced in dealing with the buyers to this point. We were happy, they were happy, and the real-estate agent was ecstatic.

Never in a million years would I have thought to ask for the affirmation of a beautiful termite treatment. I bet even the great Robert Holden, who is a terrifically funny person, wouldn't have seen that coming. Everyone got a win out of it, and because of this, I recognized it as an affirmation. If the deal had fallen through, it still would have been for the good of us all, but I probably wouldn't have recognized it as an affirmation or realized that we can experience affirmations in many ways. Affirmations are tools of the mind that take form in our lives. If our thinking categorizes life and circumstances as good or bad, then we limit the ways that affirmations have a positive effect. If we open our lives to how everything is for us, then the affirmations have unlimited ways in which to enrich our lives, as evidenced by how a termite treatment can beautifully, personally, and positively affirm life.

Affirmation Inquiry

1. Are there ways in which recent challenges or disappointments opened room for affirmation?

2. How is or has life been affirming you?

3. What do you need affirmed?

4.

Notes

_____

_____

_____

_____

_____

_____

_____

_____

_____

_____

_____

_____

_____

_____

_____

_____

_____

_____

_____

_____

_____

29

Expectations

We often don't realize the expectations we have for ourselves, for other people, and for relationships. But we can experience disappointment and hurt when our expectations aren't met. We can carry forward the stories that come from that past disappointment into the present, darkly coloring the relationships and our quality of life. But it doesn't have to happen that way, as I found out thanks to my dad.

When I was little, my dad was the tickle monster. He made us laugh until it hurt. He was the man who played with us for hours in the swimming pool. He was a disciplinarian who spanked us with the intent to raise us with rules and a moral code. He was the one with major depression and some serious religious-guilt issues.

As the oldest child, I had a rocky relationship with him. I so wanted to please him. I wanted to be good enough for him. But it wasn't his way to reward the good. We analyzed the bad so that we could improve. His disciplinarian mentality clashed with my fierce independence. But he really did the best he could. He was raised the way he raised me. Many of the things he tried out on me went by the wayside by the fourth child. He once told me that the reason my youngest sister turned out so well is because he had nothing to do with raising her. Yes, that could be construed as offensive to me. That never crossed his mind. He was negative toward himself and never once thought of how that would come across to his oldest child. I loved him dearly, but I was never able to maintain a close relationship with him. I never did feel good enough for him.

My dad was one of my greatest teachers on this earth. I had to learn how to self-nurture, how to stand up for myself, how to forgive, how to have courage, and how to love when you have disappointment. I so much wanted to have that wonderful father–daughter relationship you hear so much about. It wasn't to be, and I agonized over that.

One day, I realized that all my thoughts around my dad were awful and the cause of much of my suffering. I was tired of thinking the same things about him. Telling the same stories over and over made me miserable. I just didn't want to hear it from myself any longer. *Finally*, I was done with that. I had to do something drastic, so I killed him—in my mind. This awful Italian accent resounded in my mind, saying, "You are dead to me! I kill you! You are dead to me!" In essence, I killed *my story and expectations* of my dad and our relationship to that point. I killed every expectation and every disappointment I held. I buried them all. I spat on the grave.

Then, I left it alone. With a bit of time, I began to answer his calls without hesitation. Each interaction was its own interaction. I didn't put it on top of all the ones we had in the past. Those expectations of what we could have been and weren't were dead and buried. Eventually, I began initiating a call or a visit. We were reborn in a new relationship, one without a story or even expectations of what we should be now. We both needed the healing this different relationship had to offer. Every time I picked up the phone when he called, I was filled with grace instead of anger, grace instead of frustration, and grace instead of disappointment. For a while, we had the story of today. That was until he lost his mind from dementia and then passed away on Christmas Day.

I am so grateful to have been able to kill the expectations of him and us before he passed away, because now, no regrets about our relationship cloud my memory of our family's very own tickle monster.

Expectations Inquiry

1. What expectations that you have set for yourself or others leave you disappointed or hurt?

2. What stories are you ready to kill?

3. How would you feel without the stories or expectations? How do you feel knowing you have control of your expectations?

4.

Notes

_____

_____

_____

_____

_____

_____

_____

_____

_____

_____

_____

_____

_____

_____

_____

_____

_____

_____

Differences

Thanks to my job, I have had wonderful opportunities to meet people from all over the world, from many different walks of life, and with many different careers. I know firsthand how meeting people different from yourself can enrich your life experience. As a person who is seeking peace, violence is not a solution I choose. But I have plenty of friends who are in the military, and they have trained hard and lived a life where violent action for both defense and offense is not only a viable and necessary option but a frame of mind. Most of these friends are highly trained, dedicated, and loyal. Several of them are highly philosophical, and I have had many pleasurable conversations with them on the nature of life, reality, and service.

One of these friends was a military sniper—a really good one. He came back from active duty and pledged himself to a life of prevention in the area of homeland security, rather than a life of targeted response. He has never said that he regretted his position as sniper. I don't think it would be fair to even assume that. I believe that he was proud of his skill but not proud of taking lives in the way he had been obligated.

What I found so interesting was that I had never felt safer in someone's presence. He exuded both confidence and competence. It really fascinated me that we could talk about deep and real subjects because he had faced life-and-death situations. Nothing was off-limits, and everything was completely honest. It was refreshing to say the least. He had his demons, as we all do. But he was unique, and kind, and real.

I once called him long distance from a training I was participating in. One of our instructors had just had a long discussion with us in the bar about his service and what his unit had sacrificed. It hit me very deeply about what some people choose to do, what some are forced to do, and what others like me tend to presume about it. I had some guilt about it. So, I called my friend to discuss it, and he told me something that set me free. He said, "Brigid, I was meant to do what I did. It is as simple as that. For all of history, there has been a warrior class, medical personnel, scholars and teachers, and the like. I was meant for the warrior class. You were meant to do what you are doing."

How insightful. I would have missed that entirely if he had not been available, not been my friend, and not been so clear about himself. He may think of himself as a warrior, but I also know him to be a teacher and philosopher. We are very different, as we should be. He did not judge me for not enlisting, as I have not judged him for enlisting.

Life's diversity makes it interesting. We are all designed differently, and either we can make that out to be a problem, or we can embrace it and we can learn from it, leverage it, and become all the better for it. Through others' experiences, we can learn vicariously rather than learn every painful lesson personally. By embracing others' experiences, we can also revel in their joys. These are certainly blessings not to be taken for granted.

Differences Inquiry

1. What people in your life are different from you, and how have they enriched your life?

2. What would happen if you picked a person very different from yourself and struck up a conversation with them or invited them to dinner? Can you see them? Can they see you?

3.

Notes

_____

_____

_____

_____

_____

_____

_____

_____

_____

_____

_____

_____

_____

_____

_____

_____

_____

_____

_____

_____

Patience

Life is constantly unfolding. My worst fault is impatience, and I have received many opportunities over my lifetime to learn what patience is for and to learn how to trust life to deliver what is needed when it is needed. My art has served me in so many ways, especially in developing patience. It has been my lesson and my reward.

For example, when I was first learning the fine art of graphite pencil drawing, I told my best friend that I really wanted to learn to draw eyes. Animal eyes are particularly appealing since they can be so different and so expressive—windows to the soul, most certainly. (And being a veterinarian, I thought it seemed like an extension of my profession.) In a way, it would be blending art and science, as well as balancing my left brain and right brain. And well, hell, it would be fun to produce something of beauty that expressed my love and appreciation of animals.

Almost immediately after that conversation, I saw an artist on the internet selling DVDs on how to draw eyes. Life showed me a resource, and I followed up on it. Amazingly, the artist was a really good teacher, and I was able to draw eyes pretty well. So then I wanted to draw fur. All of a sudden, this same artist/teacher had a four-disc DVD set on how to draw hair. Ask and ye shall receive. Using this drawing technique, I drew portraits of several shelter animals. Then, in December 2014, this same artist/teacher released a teaching series on how to draw a cat with colored eyes. His teaching series to that point had always just been about graphite. I knew I had to get it, but I did not feel a strong desire to do the lessons.

In January 2015, Tom Thompson, photographer for the veterinary school I graduated from, posted two pictures of his cat online—one in color and one in black and white. I immediately saw in my mind an overlay of those two pictures—a graphite cat with colored eyes. I contacted Tom and asked for permission to draw from his pictures. He, thankfully, gave his permission. I drew the cat, Tiger Lily, in black and white with colored eyes while simultaneously doing the lessons I had purchased a month earlier.

I then submitted the picture to the *Journal of the American Veterinary Medical Association* (*JAVMA*) for consideration as cover art. Two weeks later, on April Fool's Day to be exact, they asked me if they could use it for their June 15 issue. Learning to draw an art piece worthy of cover art took me about five years. Actually doing the drawing that I submitted took me only two and a half months of working on it part-time (since I have other full-time work).

Submitting art to *JAVMA* had been on my bucket list. I had no idea when or how that would happen. But as soon as I saw those two pictures as one whole, I *knew* that it was the art piece I would submit. I am so thankful for the opportunity to have a piece of art out there in the world for others to appreciate. And I have great gratitude and not a small bit of awe for how this came to be.

Each step, each decision to move forward is getting us to where we need to be. We need not see the end of the path if we can trust that each step is leading us right to where we need to go to realize our intentions. It is easier now for me to be patient since I know that each step forward is leading me where I need to go. Patience has also become its own reward since I am able to enjoy the process rather than push for a finish for which I may not be prepared. Patience (through much practice) has become my pacemaker for arrival at successful outcomes. A very important lesson for me regarding patience is that I often don't know how it has paid off until I look back and see how things have unfolded. Patience—or impatience, as it may be—often cultivates wisdom.

Patience Inquiry

1. In what ways have you experienced patience and impatience?

2. When have you met a challenge that required patience? What did you learn?

3. Looking back, how has patience or impatience served you?

4.

Notes

_____

_____

_____

_____

_____

_____

_____

_____

_____

_____

_____

_____

_____

_____

_____

_____

_____

_____

_____

_____

Value

Animals in a barnyard overheard one farmer talking to another farmer over the fence. The cow turned to the other animals. "They said cows are worth over $400 million in this state," she said.

The chickens laughed. "Well, they said we're worth $2 billion."

The dog turned to walk out of the barn. Just before walking out the door, he looked back to retort, "Well, the farmer's wife said I am priceless."

The idea of how much value something has continually fascinates me. It really is all in the eye of the beholder. Take our perception of animals. I have a very good friend who has pictures of her cows on her computer as a screen saver. One day, I commented on how much I liked one cow picture. She said, "Oh, that's Bessie. She's hamburger now."

Then take my mother, who is vegetarian and sleeps with both her dogs plastered to her side, each trying to be the one closest to her. She often won't leave the house if there is a threat of a storm because one of the dogs gets nervous. My mother will completely upend her schedule to accommodate this little animal.

But look at how we handle other things: How many men baby their cars? How often do women covet their jewelry? A child's handmade ornament is often precious to their parents.

How much we value things may be directly related to how attached we are to them and what our story about them is—who they belonged to, where we were when we obtained them, who made them, whether the person or animal associated with the items is dead or alive, or whether others value them and so confer status for us.

But the ultimate lesson here is in the idea of value and that it can be defined differently for different people and that it can be a very personal thing. Understanding that has led me to be more cautious about judgments and has opened space within me to allow others to have their own assessment of value. After all, everything has value in some way, or else we wouldn't cling so tightly to ideas and things. Even the stuff we judge as bad must have some value or purpose to it, or else it wouldn't be an issue. I often ask myself, "What purpose does this have to me?" It is just another way of saying, "In what ways do I value this?" Interestingly, this has led me to release a lot of things from my experience. For instance, there was a time when I valued others' opinion of me. Then, I realized that others' opinion of me has absolutely nothing to do with me. It is their business, not mine.

I was able to release the attachment I had to pleasing others because I valued my peace more than I valued that which I could not control. But I must say that releasing the need to please was harder than letting go of the bikinis and perms I loved when I was twenty-one years old, which also have no value for me now.

Value Inquiry

1. What do you value most? How do you know this?

2. What determines your value?

3. Do you find what you valued in the past precious? Why or why not?

4.

Notes

_____

_____

_____

_____

_____

_____

_____

_____

_____

_____

_____

_____

_____

_____

_____

_____

_____

_____

_____

Too Much

Spontaneous laughter bubbled up and just exploded out of my mouth. Then I couldn't stop giggling—at the thought and then the situation. It really wasn't that funny, but I couldn't help laughing. Embarrassing but also heartwarming, the looks on the faces of the other people in the group just made it all the more funny.

There were seven of us sitting in a circle. We were having an ongoing discussion about what we had experienced in that morning's meditations. Up to that point, I hadn't said a word. Then all of a sudden, I had an outburst of giggling—really not like me at all.

The last comment I had heard was "We are enough just as we are right now." I had heard and read this sentiment many, many times before. This was not a new idea. Neither was the long-held, underlying belief that I was never enough.

But I had suddenly remembered an interview Tami Simon, the publisher of Sounds True, had with Eckhart Tolle, the German-born spiritual teacher and author of *The Power of Now*. He related a story in which someone had asked him, "What is your greatest achievement in life?" He said to them, "I don't need to think anymore unless I want to think. That's my achievement." Then he said, "But that's not really an achievement because it is a negative thing, it's a non." He hadn't added to anything; incessant thought had been removed from his experience. He was, in essence, back to his authentic being. Thoughts came to him when needed, but the constant chatter that had been happening had disappeared.

I couldn't help giggling. It struck me so forcefully that all my life, I had felt like I was not enough, but really, I may have been too much. I had done my level best to learn, grow, and achieve more. Maybe I should have been letting go, releasing, and being. Positive psychology and new spiritual thinking reinforce that we are already enough right now as we are. Eckhart Tolle's interview reinforced this new perspective. Maybe what is really happening is we are *too much*.

If we live in "an uncompromising acceptance of what is," as Eckhart Tolle teaches, can we live in peace not only with the external situations as a complete now but also with the "what is" right now at the heart of our existence—the already enoughness, no more need to achieve? Easier said than done, I know.

Maybe if we let go of the adding to and allowed the undoing of the walls, the angers, the hatreds, the frustrations, the constant craving for progress, and the incessant thoughts, we would relax and allow a natural removal of obstacles and walls. In essence, we would cease being too much. Maybe this would allow us to be. Be the enough that we already are; be as we have been created—a manifestation and expression of love—which, in my experience, may induce giggling.

Too Much Inquiry

1. In what ways have you been too much? How can you give yourself a break?

2. How would it feel if you just stopped striving?

3. How are you already enough? How might you accept yourself right now?

4. Is your sense of self based on achievement? Why?

5.

Notes

_____

_____

_____

_____

_____

_____

_____

_____

_____

_____

_____

_____

_____

_____

_____

_____

_____

_____

34

Soul

My soul is your soul.

Our souls are God's soul.

I reach for joy, and we expand.

When I feel bad, you are not there.

But I am not afraid because

I know to listen for you calling me

Back to where the Spirit rejoices.

Soul Inquiry

1. What is your concept or experience of God?

2. Is your concept of God different from your concept of yourself?

3. Is your concept of God or yourself different from love or joy?

4.

Notes

_____

_____

_____

_____

_____

_____

_____

_____

_____

_____

_____

_____

_____

_____

_____

_____

_____

_____

_____

_____

35

The Right Decision

When you are sorrowful, look again in your heart, and you shall see that in truth you are weeping for that which has been your delight.

—Kahlil Gibran

Our Labrador, Luke, was put to sleep about three months ago. I adopted him while still in veterinary school. He is the reason I believe in love at first sight. Picture liquid brown eyes, silky black fur, and huggable sweetness. He loved three things—us, a ball, and food, not necessarily in that order.

One evening, we came home and found him lying on the deck, unable to get up. I knew it was time to make the decision when he wouldn't eat. That is a bad sign for any dog but especially for a Lab. His hips had been bad for years, and when his time came, he let us know. I will always be thankful to him for that. Other pets have not given me such an obvious sign.

People often struggle to decide what to do when beloved pets get old and lose their quality of life. Veterinarians struggle with the same decisions that all pet owners face. In my experience, our pets are thankful for our care and trust us to decide what feels right. They don't hold grudges or impose guilt, and thankfully, they lack our inadequacies. The reason we love them so is because they love so purely. They do not live with regret, resentment, or guilt. They do not project into the future and wish for things to be different, nor do they experience a fear of death. They are the definition of living in the present. They may have fear in the present from things like thunderstorms, but when it ends, it ends.

As their guardians, we struggle over whether we should have them euthanized, whether there is a right time, and how we can deal with our deep sadness. It never occurs to them to worry about any of that. As a veterinarian and pet owner, I can only say that if you do struggle with these issues, then you most certainly are doing the right thing, no matter what you decide. It represents your courage to love and do the best for your companion. And if you do not struggle with these issues and are at peace with your decision, you are also doing the right thing. Your companion would never want you to experience suffering over relieving theirs. That's why there is no wrong decision. Whatever decision we make, it is the right one.

I have come to realize that relieving suffering and letting go can be an act of love. Though pets may experience the physical pain of their disease at the time of euthanasia, I truly believe the only emotion they experience is love. Why? Because when dogs hear the voice or feel the touch of their owner at the time of euthanasia, I have seen them attempt to wag their tail! It may be brief and weak, but it's there. If their tail doesn't work or they have no tail, then they may show love in their eyes or through a brief lick of the hand. That's all they ever really seem to want—to be with us until they are not. Well, that and some peanut butter. That is all we need to remember because that is what makes the memories so sweet.

The Right Decision Inquiry

1. In what ways or instances have your sorrows been your delight?

2. How does dealing with the death of a pet help us deal with the concept of our own death?

3. When have you struggled with letting go, and how have you managed that?

4.

Notes

_____

_____

_____

_____

_____

_____

_____

_____

_____

_____

_____

_____

_____

_____

_____

_____

_____

_____

_____

_____

_____

Perfect Day

Today has been the perfect day. The beautiful thing about it is that nothing extraordinary happened. Yesterday, my mother and I had a long talk about what being "free" means. I told her that to me, it means not having depression, dropping defenses, being at peace, feeling love, and being able to express that love without fear.

Then today, for the first time in as long as I can remember, I did not have any looming deadlines, and I am caught up. So pressure from work was not present. My kids are not in school, so they were not stressed, and my husband had a meeting in another town, so he was out of the house early. Because of all these things, it was like time was standing still just for me. I deeply expressed my thanks to life for such a moment and promised that I would make the most of it.

In that gratitude, I just breathed. I made myself aware of how it felt to breathe deeply without pressure inside or out. I spent time in meditation, committing this moment to memory. I petted the dog and the cats. I ate lunch with my son. I did some art. I just lived in the now of the day. Then I wrote this all down so I could remember just how it felt to flow through a day without effort.

And then I was thankful again and again for just now and for having a memory blueprint for creating more perfect days.

Perfect Day Inquiry

1. What is your idea of a perfect day?

2. When was the last time you enjoyed "no effort"?

3. When do you feel most free? When did you last feel free?

4.

Notes

_____

_____

_____

_____

_____

_____

_____

_____

_____

_____

_____

_____

_____

_____

_____

_____

_____

_____

_____

_____

37

Zebras

All animals fascinate me. However, I am attracted to animals ordained in black and white. Maybe that same attraction led me to pick up graphite pencils. I like the range of values and the contrast of black against white. My drawing of zebras was inspired by a photo taken by Tom Thompson. He and his family were on vacation in Africa when he shot the original photo. Tom has given me blanket permission to draw from his photos. I am most thankful for that because it is extremely helpful to have a really good photo for inspiration.

When I saw this picture, I immediately fell in love with it for several reasons. I loved the challenge of it. At first, you see a lot of lines. Drawing that alone will make you a better artist. But the other thing that adds to the photo's dimension is the many layers of animals to try to make distinctive; the out-of-focus animals behind the focal animal, the texture of the fur and the hair, and the angle of the light all made for a very interesting study.

But the ultimate reason for choosing this particular photo was to pay tribute to the beautiful animals themselves. They are gorgeous; surprisingly, no two are alike. They are known for their power and orneriness. They have gumption. There are a lot of beautiful animals. There are a lot of funny animals. There are a lot of animals with raw power. But there are not a lot of animals with beauty and gumption. Zebras have all that and more.

This one picture illustrates how to stand out from a crowd by exhibiting both beauty and gumption. No frills. Just being.

Zebras Inquiry

1. Where do you feel most comfortable—blending into the background or being a point of focus? Why?

2. How can you find simultaneous acceptance of your individuality and your place among many? How can you celebrate both?

3. Who do you know who is spiritually beautiful and has gumption? Can you find those traits within yourself?

4.

Notes

_____

_____

_____

_____

_____

_____

_____

_____

_____

_____

_____

_____

_____

_____

_____

_____

_____

_____

38

Divorce

The word *divorce*, like the words *God* and *love*, has very different connotations to different people. Some people equate divorce with freedom, and others equate it with failure, while others see it merely as a necessary step from one relationship to another. I really never thought I would have to figure it out for myself, but that is what happened. As it turned out, our divorce defined itself. We could never have predicted how it unfolded.

It was quite a shock to find out that after twenty-four years of marriage and thirty years together, both my husband and I wanted a divorce, even though, throughout our marriage, we often seemed out of sync. There were times he seemed to love me more than I loved him, and then vice versa. Yet the divorce discussion happened so in sync it was obvious that this was the next step in the evolution of our relationship. Looking back, I could see how we had been slowly but surely unraveling.

It happened in such a surreal manner. There was no screaming or yelling. There was no blame or recrimination. In fact, we had gone away for a weekend together. The day had been pleasant, and we were having an evening glass of wine in a casino bar while we played video poker on the same machine. My husband was rubbing my back and leaning into me as I said, "You don't seem happy anymore. Do you want to talk about divorce?" He stopped still and looked at me sheepishly. Then he said the words that ended the marriage phase of our life together: "I am glad you brought it up."

Just like that, everything changed and nothing changed at all. For the next two days of our getaway, we talked about how we wanted to take care of each other in this, how we wanted to be kind, how much we wanted to take care of our children, and how we intended to remain a family. We discussed our feelings. I cried *a lot*. We had goodbye sex. We apologized for disappointing each other and letting each other down. But we tried not to go too far down that road because we didn't want to cheapen or negate what we had built in all our years together. Neither of us wanted to leave our marriage with a sense of regret. We knew that weekend that what we built had been meant to be, and that now it was time to support each other in doing something different.

Changing thirty years of togetherness into separate lives with common interests has not been all smooth sailing. It sometimes angers me that he moved an hour and a half away from me and the kids so the kids don't see him but about once a week. Yet I know that there is a higher purpose for that. It may be so that we can make a clean break. It may be so that I won't always depend on him so much. It may be so that absence makes the heart grow fonder. It may be "manopause." Whatever it is really doesn't matter since this is how it is. Now, I get to choose how to respond to this circumstance. I want him to be happy. I want me to be happy. Neither of those things is possible if we have anger between us. Sure, I'd rather him be closer, but when he left, he left the kids with me. I wouldn't change one thing about having the kids with me until they are ready to leave. So, there it is. We don't have to fight over them. They don't have to choose between us. I know and they know that he loves them. That's what matters most.

I am one week away from my divorce being final. Both my teenage children are home, resting and happy. Tomorrow, they will see their father, and I will see my friend. A week and a half from now, I will not be married, but I will still have a family and a highly valued friendship that took me thirty years to cultivate. So, through the divorce process, we have defined a new normal. Our divorce has defined us as no longer married but forever friends and family.

Divorce Inquiry

1. What major changes have taken place in your life?

2. What current situations or responses can you redefine for your own happiness?

3. What is your deepest intent, and is it reflected in your choices?

4.

Notes

_____

_____

_____

_____

_____

_____

_____

_____

_____

_____

_____

_____

_____

_____

_____

_____

_____

_____

_____

39

Be-er

There comes a time when you have to *be* what you are. For most of my life, I have been an active seeker of information, knowledge, and answers. I remember one summer, a fellow participant in a course I was taking looked at me and proclaimed, "You are a seeker!" Smiling somewhat wryly, I answered, "Yes, but at some point, a seeker needs to find what they are looking for."

If one doesn't find what one is looking for, one gets very disappointed. Is that an understatement or a statement of the obvious? Regardless, it brings up the question of whether you can be both a seeker and a finder. I guess it is possible if you begin seeking the answers to other questions. So, can you seek and *be* at the same time? That answer is not quite so obvious. If seeking something is the goal, then I think not. If being is the goal and seeking comes from that, then I think it may indeed be possible. The challenging aspect of this is the continual process of growth through experience as we move through our life journeys. As we learn and grow, we have new questions that arise. The seeking and answering of these questions can lead us to new adventures and new discoveries. We can still *be* an ever-evolving self. Yet our essence remains the same. It can be covered or uncovered, but it remains constant and steady.

So what is my essence? Who and what am I really? That has been my long-term seeker question. It has been with me for as long as I can remember, and I am not truly sure if I am closer to the answer. That is not true. The process of writing, drawing, and breathing today has gotten me closer to understanding myself. I hesitate to proclaim this is what I am because I know tomorrow, I may be seeking yet another answer to an impossibly nebulous question. But at my essence, what I really know to be true is there is the love of and love for all things. It is not something I can express at all times under all circumstances. That state of constancy may be what I am truly seeking. That isn't an answer to a question, though, is it? That is a state of being. So maybe you can't *be* and seek at the same time, not because it isn't possible to conceptualize it in words but because it happens at two different levels. Being is a state; seeking is an activity. Being assumes there is already completeness in the moment. Seeking implies there is more to grasp and know, and there is an element of time.

My sense is that seeking will end with just being. Then the *be*-er will just simply enjoy beer, and everything else for that matter. How much beer is necessary for one's individual enjoyment to then become one's quest? Who knows? I don't expect there to be the same sense of urgency in seeking the answer to that question.

Be-**er Inquiry**

1. Are you a seeker? Are you a *be*-er?

2. In what ways does your seeking contribute to your being?

3. So what is your essence? Who and what are you really?

4. If you were a beer, what kind would you be?

5.

Notes

_____

_____

_____

_____

_____

_____

_____

_____

_____

_____

_____

_____

_____

_____

_____

_____

_____

_____

_____

_____

HOMEWARD BOUND

When I started this book, I wondered how I would end it. I wondered if I would be able to report that I had arrived home or had awakened or had at least had some marvelously profound insight. But this book ends like most of the personal insights in this book—with a subtle "aha."

Today, my coworkers and I loaded up my car for a return trip to Mississippi from College Station, Texas. We had been at a weeklong conference and now were brain-dead. We had carpooled in my vehicle, so I settled into the driver's seat once again. Ronnie, my friend and coworker, offered to drive, but I automatically said (without thinking), "I got this. I can always find my way home."

And so I have.

Although we all have to find our own paths home, we don't have to ride alone. We can validate and encourage each other along the way. We can really see each other, and ourselves, with kindness and compassion. Life is a team sport. All we need to do is start where we are by looking at our lives as gifts stuffed full of messages and signs meant just for us. In return, this perspective will show us how to live our best and most fulfilled, meaningful, and joyful lives.

GUIDELINES FOR GROUP DISCUSSION

The format of this book is designed for individual self-reflection. However, the essays could easily be used for group discussion. Interesting discoveries can happen within the context of a group, especially when we can trust ourselves and allow ourselves to be vulnerable. Groups can be as small as two people, but I recommend that they not be larger than five to seven people. This will allow each person an opportunity to participate. Setting up the right environment, building and maintaining trust, and truly listening and allowing people to speak from their own sets of circumstances are dynamics that contribute to a positive group experience.

The following guidelines will foster a group environment of trust and acceptance so that truly beneficial discussion can take place.

- **Set boundaries.** Do this early on by agreeing that all discussions held within the group will be confidential. Agree that group members will not repeat information shared within the group to people outside the group who were not part of the discussion.
- **Identify a facilitator.** Group discussions involving the essays do not require a leader to direct or teach content. However, a facilitator can help ensure that all group members have an opportunity to speak if desired, as well as ensure that no one person is directing, advising, analyzing, or teaching other group members.
- **Actively listen.** This helps people feel seen and heard. It is extremely healing to be present for people. Seeing and hearing each other is a great gift that we can give through this process.
- **Choose a format.** Group members can choose to work on the same essay, or each person can pick an essay that calls to him or her. There is no right or wrong way to work with the essays. Group members can choose randomly from throughout the book, or they can read the essays in order, from front to back or back to front.
- **Do self-introspection first.** I highly recommend that each person have adequate time to read an essay and do self-introspection and journaling before beginning group discussion. Each person has his or her own inner work and inner guide. Group discussion enhances the potential to gain valuable insight, but the most valuable insight for the individual comes from each person's own life.
- **Ask open-ended questions.** Questions from one group member to another can be helpful, but it is best to keep the questions as open-ended as possible. Attempts to lead, direct, educate, advise, or analyze can change the dynamic of the group so that there is less comfort in sharing.
- **Be kind to yourself and others.** Each person's personal experience is valid, and you are your own best teacher.
- **Have fun.** Laugh alone or with group members. Laughter is healing and promotes openness.
- **Give-and-take.** Group discussions are opportunities for give-and-take. All members should be encouraged to give of themselves by listening and by speaking when comfortable.
- **Be conscientious.** Begin and end on time. During the discussion, allow each person an opportunity to speak and then truly listen while someone else is talking. The most precious gift we can give someone is our presence.

ACKNOWLEDGMENTS

How in the world do you say thank you to the people who walk with you through the most meaningful aspects of existence? How do you thank the people who help you grow, love you, and accept you as you are? A book acknowledgment is certainly not enough, but I will do my best to express my heartfelt gratitude to those who helped make this book happen.

Scott Jennings and Martina Sciolino, you were instrumental in bringing this book to fruition. Without your support and encouragement, this would not have happened. Thank you for believing in me and in this process. Thank you for loving me through it.

Thank you, Susan Nodurft, for being a sounding board, a light in the dark, and the foundation on which I launch myself into the world. I am so grateful for your support and for your friendship.

Susan Bone, thank you for your steadfastness and your willingness to embrace this labor of love. You gave me courage to keep going. I sincerely appreciate your ability to ask just the right questions but also patiently wait for the answers.

Beth Adcock, thank you ever so much for generously offering me your sharp eyes and quick wit. You are always my reassurance that things are ready to be shared.

Leanna, Honor, and Vince, you have helped me grow and given me so many important, life-affirming opportunities to discover myself through my interactions with you. You have been my treasured teachers, healers, and muses.

Thank you to all the people at Balboa Press who have been persistent and have held my hand through this process. I could not have had better guides.

THEME INDEX

	Perfect Day	108
Fear	Anguish	77
	Beauty	6
	Choices	15
	Freedom	64
	Good or Bad	45
	Left Turns	55
	Phases	23
Flow	Beauty	6
	Freedom	64
	Home	12
	Left Turns	55
	Perfect Day	108
Forgiveness	Divorce	115
	Expectations	87
	True Love	42
Freedom	Alive	50
	Beauty	6
	Differences	90
	Exuberance	80
	Freedom	64
	Intention	33
	Perfect Day	108
	Quiet Support	10
Grace	Comfort	52
	Exuberance	80
Gratitude	Being Seen	40
	Expectations	87
	Exuberance	80
	Love by Choice	36
	Patience	93
	Perfect Day	108
Healing	Expectations	87
	Good or Bad	45
	Perspectives	8
	Resistance to Assistance	74
Help	Left Turns	55
	Questions	4
Home	Home	12

	True Love	42
Life Force	Alive	50
	Exuberance	80
	Freedom	64
	More Than a Body	59
	Questions	4
	Value	97
Loss	Cardinals	19
	Divorce	115
	More Than a Body	59
	The Right Decision	105
Love	*Be*-er	118
	Cardinals	19
	Comfort	52
	Divorce	115
	Love by Choice	36
	Religion	27
	The Right Decision	105
	Soul	102
	True Love	42
Patience	Affirmation	83
	Light Switch	30
	Patience	93
	Questions	4
Peace	*Be*-er	118
	Comfort	52
	Divorce	115
	Expectations	87
	Left Turns	55
	Perfect Day	108
	Quiet Support	10
	Too Much	100
Perception	Affirmation	83
	Differences	90
	Divorce	115
	Feeding the Good Wolf	67
	Good or Bad	45
	More Than a Body	59
	Perspectives	8

	Phases	23
	Questions	4
Release	Alive	50
	Be-er	118
	Expectations	87
	Exuberance	80
	Freedom	64
	The Right Decision	105
	Soul	102
	Too Much	100
	Value	97
Risk	Freedom	64
	Left Turns	55
	Phases	23
Safety	Left Turns	55
	Phases	23
	Questions	4
Seeker or Searcher	*Be*-er	118
	Phases	23
	Questions	4
Self	Phases	23
	Sadness and a Good Life	48
	Soul	102
Self-Criticism	Expectations	87
	Home	12
Serendipity	Cardinals	19
	Choices	15
	Divorce	115
	Patience	93
	Questions	4
Signs	Cardinals	19
	Good or Bad	45
	Patience	93
	Zebras	112
Simplicity	Alive	50
	Freedom	64
	Perfect Day	108
	Soul	102
	Too Much	100

	True Love	42
	Value	97
	Zebras	112
Visibility	Being Seen	40
	Differences	90
	Learning by Example	71
	More Than a Body	59
	Perspectives	8
	Resistance to Assistance	74
	Vulnerability	2
Vulnerability	Anguish	77
	Divorce	115
	Good or Bad	45
	Left Turns	55
	Resistance to Assistance	74
	Soul	102
	Vulnerability	2

ABOUT THE AUTHOR

Brigid was born in New Orleans, Louisiana and has lived most of her life in Mississippi. She currently lives in Hattiesburg, Mississippi with her two children and two pets - who provide endless opportunities for joy and growth. Brigid has been a public practice nurse for 30 years and a public practice veterinarian for 20 years. She has many interests, ranging from writing and drawing to yoga and walking. Her life's journey has been dedicated to honest and faithful inquiry as it led her from the study of science to the study of spirit. Brigid considers life itself the essential spiritual self-study course.

Printed in the United States
By Bookmasters